Accounts of China and India

Letter from the General Editor

LIBRARY OF المكتبة ARABIC العربية LITERATURE

The Library of Arabic Literature series offers Arabic editions and English translations of significant works of Arabic literature, with an emphasis on the seventh to nineteenth centuries. The Library of Arabic Literature thus includes texts from the pre-Islamic era to the cusp of the modern period, and encompasses a wide range of genres, including poetry, poetics, fiction, religion, philosophy, law, science, history, and historiography.

Books in the series are edited and translated by internationally recognized scholars and are published in parallel-text format with Arabic and English on facing pages, and are also made available as English-only paperbacks.

The Library encourages scholars to produce authoritative, though not necessarily critical, Arabic editions, accompanied by modern, lucid English translations. Its ultimate goal is to introduce the rich, largely untapped Arabic literary heritage to both a general audience of readers as well as to scholars and students.

The Library of Arabic Literature is supported by a grant from the New York University Abu Dhabi Institute and is published by NYU Press.

Philip F. Kennedy
General Editor, Library of Arabic Literature

About this Paperback

This paperback edition differs in a few respects from its dual-language hardcover predecessor. Because of the compact trim size the pagination has changed, but paragraph numbering has been retained to facilitate cross-referencing with the hardcover. Material that referred to the Arabic edition has been updated to reflect the English-only format, and other material has been corrected and updated where appropriate. For information about the Arabic edition on which this English translation is based and about how the LAL Arabic text was established, readers are referred to the hardcover.

Accounts of China and India

BY

Abū Zayd al-Sīrāfī

TRANSLATED BY

Tim Mackintosh-Smith

FOREWORD BY

Zvi Ben-Dor Benite

VOLUME EDITOR

Philip F. Kennedy

NEW YORK UNIVERSITY PRESS
New York

NEW YORK UNIVERSITY PRESS
New York

Library of Congress Cataloging-in-Publication Data
Names: Sirafi, Abu Zayd Hasan ibn Yazid, active 10th century author. | Mackintosh-Smith, Tim, 1961– translator. | Ben-Dor Benite, Zvi author of introduction.
Title: Accounts of China and India / by Abu Zayd Al-Sirafi ; translated by Tim Macintosh-Smith ; foreword by Zvi Ben-Dor Benite.
Other titles: Silsilat al-tawarikh. English.
Description: New York : New York University Press, 2017. | Includes bibliographical references and index.
Identifiers: LCCN 2016040524 (print) | LCCN 2016042538 (ebook) | ISBN 9781479830596 (pb : alk. paper) | ISBN 9781479862054 (e-book) | ISBN 9781479814428 (e-book)
Subjects: LCSH: China—Description and travel—Early works to 1800. | India—Description and travel—Early works to 1800.
Classification: LCC DS409 .S5713 2017 (print) | LCC DS409 (ebook) | DDC 915.104—dc23
LC record available at https://lccn.loc.gov/2016040524

New York University Press books are printed on acid-free paper, and their binding materials are chosen for strength and durability.

Series design and composition by Nicole Hayward
Typeset in Adobe Text

Manufactured in the United States of America

10 9 8 7 6 5 4 3 2 1

MIX
Paper | Supporting responsible forestry
FSC® C013604

In memory of my aunt, Elsie Florence Harrison, who showed me the way that led to Arabia, India, and China

Contents

Foreword

ZVI BEN-DOR BENITE

The Indian Ocean has been the site of travel, trade, war, and above all, transregional human history for several millennia. Written and literary evidence for it can be found even in early biblical narratives about King Solomon bringing ivory from India. But only with the appearance of the *Accounts of China and India* (*Akhbār al-Ṣīn wa-l-Hind*) in the 9th and 10th centuries do we find a comprehensive account of the Indian Ocean. *Accounts* purports to be accounts about China and India, but in fact, it tells the story of the entire Indian Ocean—its shape, its geography, its shores, and the countries and cultures behind them. It is very evident that the compilers of this work conceived of it in this more expansive way since in several places the narrative presents thoughtful discussions about the different civilizations flourishing on the ocean's shores. Readers will find these discussions in various places throughout the work. In this respect *Accounts of China and India* is not merely a travelogue describing the regions between the Arab lands of the Eastern Gulf and the kingdoms of China and India. It is, rather, a world history, recounting the story of a nexus of human cultures in the 10th century.

That *Accounts of China and India* is a world history should come as no surprise. It draws on the accounts and practical experiences of Arab merchants that sailed to China and back, and is therefore one of the best examples of medieval Arab geography. Indeed, in the three centuries that followed the Arabs' inheritance and practical unification of most of the Mediterranean and West Asian worlds—from Andalusia in the west to the borders of China in the east—they engaged in many ambitious geographical projects. The aim was to write and map the geography (and the history, since the two were inseparable)—of the world as they knew it. *Accounts* can be seen as one the epitomes of this grand project. And China (*al-Ṣīn* in Arabic), located beyond the eastern boundaries of the world, occupied a special place in the geographical imagination of the Arabs. By virtue of being a place where different laws—natural, cultural, political—prevailed, narratives about travel to China challenged, almost by necessity, notions about the world the Arabs themselves inhabited and about the inhabited world generally.

But *Accounts of China and India* is not only a geographically informed meditation about the world. Based on actual stories by real merchants and travelers, it gives us vivid detailed descriptions. *Accounts* is in fact one of the earliest foreign accounts of China during the Tang dynasty and indeed the fullest and the most detailed of its time. Its importance is invaluable, not only because it mentions events such as the Huang Chao rebellion (835–884), but also, and principally, because of its detailed description of daily life in Canton, the main port city in Southern China during the Tang. We know much about the economic and commercial transformation that China underwent during the Tang dynasty, but we know much less about how foreign merchants, who played a vital role in it, experienced it. *Accounts* is unique in this regard. It tells us a great deal about the lives of foreign merchants in China—their interactions with the Chinese, the challenges they faced, and their perceptions of the place where they sojourned.

The book has a long history and is connected to an even longer and deeper one. In the early 13th century Zhao Rugua (1170–1228), the supervisor of maritime trade in Quanzhou (Zaitun)—the city rivaled Canton as the central hub of Arab mercantile activity after the 11th century—compiled the *Zhufanzhi* (*Records of Foreign Peoples*). The *Zhufanzhi* was based on stories and information provided by foreign merchants of a very similar background of those that fed *Accounts of China and India* a few centuries before. *Accounts* was probably on the mind of travelers such as the Moroccan, Ibn Baṭṭūṭah (1304–1368 or 1369), who traveled in the Indian Ocean and China during the Mongol period. During the early 15th century, when the Chinese set sail in the Indian Ocean under the admiralship of Zheng He (1371–1433 or 1435), one of their missions was to update the knowledge contained in the *Zhufanzhi*. The product of this expedition was the *Yingyai Shenglan* (*Overall Survey of the Ocean's Shores*) of the scribe Ma Huan (c. 1380–1461). It cannot be a coincidence that Ma Huan, a Chinese Muslim from the Yangzi Delta was in charge of Zheng He's mission. Ma Huan was most probably a descendant of Arab Muslim merchants that settled in China in earlier times—perhaps not as early as the time when *Accounts* was compiled, but certainly as part of the same maritime activity described in it. Famously, Zheng He, was also a Muslim.

During the early 18th century, at the height of the European Age of Sail, French, and later English, the European readership was very interested in the goings-on in an ocean that was proving important for trade and conquest. *Accounts* was one of the very first geographical accounts of the Indian Ocean to be translated into European languages. Almost three centuries after its first publication in English, and at a time when China, India, and the Indian Ocean are rising once more in global prominence, the publication of this beautiful and scholarly translation is a cause for celebration.

Zvi Ben-Dor Benite
New York University

Acknowledgments

I would like to thank in particular: my old friend Dr Ḥasan ʿAbd al-Wahhāb al-Shamāḥī of Ṣanʿāʾ, for helping me tease out some of the knottier problems of the text; Ianthe Maclagan and Tim Morris, for their wonderful hospitality in Oxford and Andalusia; Professor Zvi Ben-Dor Benite, for restoring some especially tricky arabicized Chinese terms to their original forms; the Bibliothèque Nationale de France, for supplying with remarkable speed a superb digital copy of the only known manuscript; and Philip Kennedy, Chip Rossetti, and Gemma Juan-Simó for their unceasing encouragement and editorial support from Abu Dhabi and New York. I am also indebted to the late Professor Sauvaget, whose work on the First Book of the *Accounts* was truly a labor of love, for a number of suggested readings and interpretations.

Introduction

This is a book about an ocean and the lands that lie on its shores, about the ships that cross it and the cargoes they carry. In its own words, it is a book about

> the Sea of India and China, in whose depths are pearls and ambergris, in whose rocky isles are gems and mines of gold, in the mouths of whose beasts is ivory, in whose forests grow ebony, sapan wood, rattans, and trees that bear aloewood, camphor, nutmeg, cloves, sandalwood, and all manner of fragrant and aromatic spices, whose birds are parrots and peacocks, and the creeping things of whose earth are civet cats and musk gazelles, and all the rest that no one could enumerate, so many are its blessings.[1]

It might have been the inspiration for John Masefield's quinquireme of Nineveh in his poem "Cargoes," with its

> cargo of ivory,
> And apes and peacocks,
> Sandalwood, cedarwood, and sweet white wine.

(And, yes, there is sweet white wine in this book too, made from the sap of the toddy palm.) But it is about more than that, for there is a whole human landscape: ships' captains and customs men, kings and courtiers, princes and paupers—and a few cannibals and kidnappers, to add spice.

What's more, the book describes a real, live world, almost palpably real, despite the passing of eleven centuries. It is built from facts, not sailors' yarns. As the author says in his closing words, "I have avoided relating any of the sort of accounts in which sailors exercise their powers of invention,"[2] sailors, according to his illustrious predecessor al-Jāḥiẓ, not being "respecters of the unvarnished truth. The stranger the story the more they like it; and, moreover, they use vulgar expressions and have an atrocious style."[3] Reality and solidity are what are implied by the first word of the title: *akhbār*, accounts, are reports from credible witnesses. And each *khabar*, each account, fits in with the others to be assembled into a jigsaw picture of a world not unlike our own, a world on the road to globalization.

It is a short book, but it has a sweeping perspective, from the Swahili coast to a rather mistily glimpsed Korea. It is therefore one of those books that seems bigger than it is. And, like the ports of that immense Afro-Asiatic littoral, its pages are busy with people and piled with goods, not just with the luxuries listed above but also with a priceless cargo of information, especially on China. Here are the first foreign descriptions of tea and porcelain, and a whole panorama of Chinese society, from the Son of Heaven and Confucian ethics down to toilet paper and bamboo urinals.

And all this marvelous, mundane world is contained in the compass of a novella. As its own last words say, *wa-in qalla awlā*:[4] Less is more.

Dating and Authorship

If *Accounts of China and India* is good value in its geographical and material coverage, there is a bonus: it is, in fact, two books.

Book One, according to the author of Book Two, dates to the year 237/851–52.[5] There is no reason to doubt this date, and internal evidence supports it.[6] The author of Book One, however, is unknown. It does not help that the first pages are missing from the only manuscript copy known to have survived; these might have given an author's name. Nor does it help that another writer, Ibn al-Faqīh, a writer much closer in time to the composition of Book One than we are, quoted some of its text with an attribution to one Sulaymān al-Tājir.[7] This Sulaymān the Merchant was undoubtedly one of the informants for Book One; he is the only one mentioned in it by name.[8] Commentators in search of authors have therefore leapt on Sulaymān and credited him with the whole book. It is perfectly usual in Arabic books of the time for their authors to appear in the text, as Sulaymān does, in the third person, as if I were to interject suddenly, "And Tim Mackintosh-Smith said . . ." This is, in itself, no obstacle to the attribution of authorship to Sulaymān, but it is likewise not an argument for it. Much ink has been shed over the question, but, in the end, we have no incontrovertible evidence for Sulaymān or anyone else being the author of Book One.

There is a further possible element of mystery: the author of Book One may have been unknown even to the author of Book Two. It is certainly strange that the latter, in the evaluation of Book One that forms the preamble to his own work,[9] does not say who wrote that earlier book. Later on, when he has another chance to name the author of Book One, he seems intentionally to avoid doing so: he calls him merely "the person from whom that First Book was taken down."[10] To me there seems to be only one entirely cogent reason that the author of Book Two did not mention his predecessor's name, which is that he himself did not know it.

About the author of Book Two there is no doubt. He is there at the outset, staking his third-person claim to authorship in the book's opening words, "Abū Zayd al-Ḥasan al-Sīrāfī said . . ."[11] If we knew nothing else about him, we would know from his surname that he was from—or at least had some connection with—the city of Sīrāf on the Iranian shore of the Gulf, which for much of the third/ninth and fourth/tenth centuries was the most important port for long-distance trade across the Indian Ocean. But we do know a little more, from no less an authority than the great historian-geographer al-Masʿūdī: he met Abū Zayd in Basra and says that he "had moved there from Sīrāf in the year 303 [915–16].” Al-Masʿūdī then gives a lineage for Abū Zayd (in which the names of earlier ancestors show an Iranian ethnic origin) and adds that he was “a man of discrimination and discernment,” that is, that he was a man of learning, with a well-developed critical sense.[12]

In contrast to Book One, in Book Two it is the date that is the problem. It was obviously being written well after the end of the Huang Chao rebellion in China, suppressed in 271/884, and some considerable time into the ensuing decades of anarchy; these events are reported near the beginning of the book.[13] Book Two was finished, as will become clear below, by the time al-Masʿūdī was working on his own *Meadows of Gold and Mines of Gems* (*Murūj al-dhahab wa-maʿādin al-jawhar*) in 332/943–44. But that still leaves a wide range of possible dates. We will return to the question.

There is another question to ask and to return to. Immediately after declaring his authorship, Abū Zayd says, “I have examined this foregoing book (meaning the First Book), *having been commanded* to look carefully through it, and to verify the information I find in it,” and moreover to supplement it “with other reports . . . known to myself but not appearing in the book.”[14] These supplementary accounts grew into Book Two. Abū Zayd undoubtedly wrote Book Two, but who was its instigator, the mysterious figure who commanded or instructed him to do so? If he was some important literary patron, why not commemorate him by name? Why hide him with a passive verb, the “anonymous” voice of the Arabic grammarians? Throughout Book Two, that nameless presence peers over the author’s shoulder.

Then again Abū Zayd and his predecessor, the writer of Book One, were, strictly speaking, compilers, not authors. The material of both books came from the informants who contributed their *akhbār*, their eyewitness accounts. Other than Sulaymān the Merchant and a certain Ibn Wahb, whose report of his visit to China is incorporated into Book Two,[15] they too are nameless. But these two suggest identities for the anonymous remainder. The other contributors were almost certainly merchants like Sulaymān (rather than mere yarning sailors); they were probably from the Gulf region—Ibn Wahb was from the Iraqi port city of Basra at its head—and especially from Sīrāf, that great trans-oceanic terminus. Most important, they all seem to have visited and spent time in the places they talk about. There is a glimpse of them as a group at the end of Book Two, where the writer apologizes for his lack of information on al-Sīlā (Korea): "None of our circle of informants has ever made it there and brought back a reliable report."[16] These are the true authors, this circle of ex-expatriates, old China and India hands back home, swapping memories of far-off lands like a coterie of Sindbads—and all the more wonderful for being real characters with real stories.

The Historical Context

Those merchant-informants traveled through an open world. Arab expansion—and especially what could be called the Asianization of the Arab-Islamic polity under the Abbasid dynasty from the mid-second/eighth century on—had thrown open an eastward-facing window of trade and travel. The new age is summed up in a saying attributed to al-Manṣūr, the second Abbasid caliph and builder of Baghdad. Standing on the bank of the river of the recently founded imperial city and watching the silks and porcelain unloading, he exclaimed, "Here is the Tigris, and nothing bars the way between it and China!"[17] At the same time, and at the other end of that eastward way, the Chinese were discovering new far-western horizons, with the Tang-dynasty geographer Jia Dan describing the maritime route to Wula (al-Ubullah, ancient Apologus) at the head of the Gulf, then up to Bangda (Baghdad).[18]

The hemiglobal scope of commerce comes across in the diversity of goods described in the *Accounts*: Indian rhino horn, Tibetan musk, Gulf pearls, Chinese porcelain, Sri Lankan sapphires, Maldivian coir, Arabian and East African ambergris, Abyssinian leopard skins. It also comes across in the sheer mobility of individuals mentioned—people like the merchant from Khurasan in eastern Iran, who "made his way to the land of the Arabs, and from there to the kingdoms of the Indians, and then came to [China], all in pursuit of honorable gain," in his case from selling ivory and other luxury goods. In China, his merchandise was taken illegally by an official, but his case reached the ears of the emperor, who chastised the official concerned: "You . . . wanted [this merchant] to return by way of these same kingdoms, telling everyone in them, 'I was treated unjustly in China and my property was seized by force'!"[19] By rights, the emperor said, the official should have been put to death for his action. The message is plain: bad publicity would damage China's reputation as a stable market and a serious trading partner, and that damage would spread across the whole vast continent of Asia. Then, as now, it was supply and demand that propelled and steered the ship of trade, but it was confidence that kept it afloat.

More literally, however, what drove the ships along the "maritime Silk Road" of the Indian Ocean was the great system of winds with its annual alternating cycle, taking vessels eastward in one season and back west in another—the Arabic for "season," *mawsim*, giving English (via the Portuguese *moução/monção*) its name for that system, "monsoon."[20] The two great termini of the monsoon trade were Sīrāf in the Gulf and the Chinese city of Khānfū—which was, according to Abū Zayd, home to 120,000 foreign merchants in the later third/ninth century;[21] the ports of Kūlam Malī in southwestern India and Kalah Bār on the west coast of the Malay Peninsula were the two major havens and crucial entrepôts along the way. Of these four, Kalah Bār has never been pinpointed, while Kūlam Malī survives, sleepily, as the Keralan town of Kollam; only Khānfū remains the great emporium it was, the Chinese megalopolis of Guangzhou. As for Sīrāf, birthplace of Abū Zayd and, in a sense, of this book, it is now the site of a small village; but the village crouches on the ruins of the palaces of rich ship owners and traders, merchant princes of the monsoon who dined off the finest Chinese porcelain and whose wealth grew ever greater through that climactic third/ninth century.[22]

And then, in the last quarter of that century, disaster struck. As Abū Zayd puts it, "the trading voyages to China were abandoned and the country itself was ruined, leaving all traces of its greatness gone."[23] From 260/874 on, China was convulsed by one of those rebellions that seem to well up there every few centuries; the emperor's fears of instability came home to roost, in the heart of his palace in the Tang capital, Chang'an, captured by the rebel leader Huang Chao in 266/880. As for bad publicity, it could hardly have been worse than news of the wholesale massacre of foreign merchants in Khānfū/Guangzhou. The Gulf's direct seaborne trade with China withered away. "China," Abū Zayd goes on, "has remained in chaos down to our own times."[24] The lesser Indian trade remained, and Gulf merchants still struck deals over Chinese goods, but only at the halfway point of Kalah Bār. Book Two is haunted by the knowledge that the good old days were over.

The Literary and Cultural Context

Books of *akhbār*, oral accounts set down in writing, are very old indeed. An *akhbār* collection on the ancient Arabs attributed to the first/seventh-century ʿAbīd ibn Sharyah is, by some accounts, the oldest extant Arabic book, after the Qurʾān.[25] Moreover, the fact that this ʿAbīd was a professional storyteller demonstrates how the genre sits on the division—or maybe the elision—between spoken and written literature. And if those ancient *akhbār* had as their subject matter pre-Islamic battles and heroes, then the inspiration for the overarching theme of this book is almost equally old. Time and again, the Qurʾān tells its listeners to "go about the earth and look."[26]

Akhbār, then, are supposedly verbatim oral reportage, a secular parallel to the literature of hadith, which records the sayings and doings of the Prophet Muhammad and his Companions. And although a full-scale science of *akhbār* never developed as it did for hadith, there was some attempt at classification. Al-Masʿūdī, for example, identifies two types of oral report, those that are on everyone's tongues and those that have been passed down a chain of narrators.[27] He also neatly defines *akhbār* by what they are not: his own book is one of *khabar*, not of *baḥth* and *naẓar*—that is, it presents facts as they are reported but does not analyze them through research and investigation.[28] In other words, *akhbār*, like journalism today, were seen as the first draft of history—and, in the case of *Accounts of China and India*, of geography, ethnology, economics, zoology, and much else besides.

All this means that there is an immediacy to the information. Particularly in Book Two, there are snippets of "writerly" commentary that stitch together the patchwork of accounts, but most of the text has the feel of having been told and taken down directly. An example is the account, mentioned above, of the aggrieved merchant. First, Abū Zayd has his word as literary anchorman—"The Chinese used to monitor their own system, in the old days, that is, before its deterioration in the present time, with a rigor unheard of elsewhere"—but he then gives the nod to his informant, who launches straight into his tale: "A certain man from Khurasan . . . came to Iraq . . ."[29] And the tale spools out spontaneously, occasionally getting lost in its own subordinate clauses as we all do when we speak. To listen to these accounts is to hear the unedited voice of oral history.

"Unedited" does not mean "unrehearsed": as with all travelers' tales, the accounts had no doubt already acquired a polish in the telling and retelling. Nor is it likely to mean "verbatim," for Abū Zayd and his anonymous predecessor probably further burnished their informants' grammar, syntax, and vocabulary. Despite this, some of the language is slightly wayward. It is not bad Arabic, as the French scholar Ferrand claimed;[30] rather, it preserves features of the spoken Arabic that it represents on the page—even today, actual spoken Arabic is nearly always standardized before it goes down on paper. The multiplicity of contributors and the duality of compilers also make for occasional repetitions and very occasional contradictions.[31] Geographically and thematically, too, although the compilers did their best to organize the material, the book as a whole is no disciplined Baedeker—it has more in common, in fact, with the online, interactive travel websites of our own age—nor, of course, does it have the neatness of a discrete journey by a single traveler. Instead, it weaves the threads and fragments of many journeys together into a text that, for its size, must be one of the richest in all the literature of travel and geography.

There is a danger, with all this richness and denseness, of losing one's audience. The leaps from India to China and back, the excursions to Sarbuzah and the Islands of Silver, the sidetracks into the lives of Shaivite saddhus and *devadasi* prostitutes could all be too disorienting for readers back in Basra or Baghdad. But there are always cultural "navigation aids." Inevitably, some of them do not work for us, the readers of more than a millennium later: who, for example, were the Kanīfiyyah and the Jalīdiyyah, to whom rival Indian gangs are compared?[32] Perhaps the Sharks and the Jets of fourth/tenth-century Iraq; the precise reference seems to be lost. But there is also the enduring cultural compass of Islam and Arabdom.[33] It orients the traveler to what he sees, how he sees it, and how he reports it, and the reader to how he receives the report. It works on many levels, from the way the Chinese urinate (standing, not squatting) and why,[34] to interpretations of Buddhist iconography.[35] This constant guiding presence not only enables the traveler-traders—merchants in musk and silk and porcelain, but also in knowledge—to make cultural translations for their immediate audience back home. For us, their audience removed in time, it points not just to where those travelers got to but also to where they came from.

It also may explain a few cases in which the informants' vision is apparently distorted. An example is that of Ibn Wahb's audience with the Tang emperor. Assuming the meeting did in fact take place—and Abū Zayd, that scholar of discrimination and discernment, accepted that it did—would the emperor, in his palace at the heart of the Middle Kingdom, the navel of the civilized earth, really have viewed Baghdad, the barbarian Bangda, as the center of the world and the Abbasid caliph as above him in the international order of precedence?[36] Perhaps he (or his interpreter) was being exceedingly diplomatic. Or perhaps Ibn Wahb was doing what later, European, writers were to do, notably the author of the travels of Sir John Mandeville, in that dubious knight's even more dubious audience with the Mamluk sultan:[37] using the figure of the wise infidel king to make a point about one's own society.

There was certainly a point to be made in the third/ninth century—that the still young Arab-Islamic civilization of the West had not only joined the club of Asian cultures but had also outstripped its ancient fellow members in global importance. If this is indeed the subtext of that strange imperial pronouncement, then it is made more subtly and more eloquently, not by emperors but by unknown merchants, on every page of this book: for it is a book that tells us, by reflex, so to speak, as much about the energy and enterprise of Islam in that age as it does about China and India.

Abū Zayd and Al-Masʿūdī

Al-Masʿūdī, the Herodotus of the Arabs, as he is often and aptly called, was quoted above on Abū Zayd and on the meaning of *akhbār*. Those quotations are from his main surviving work, *Meadows of Gold and Mines of Gems*. But there is more to be said on the relationship between the two authors and their works, for significant portions of the material in *Accounts of China and India* appear also in the pages of al-Masʿūdī. Who got what from whom?

There is, of course, no question about matter taken from Book One, finished some eighty years before al-Masʿūdī was working on his *Meadows of Gold*. Regarding information appearing in our Book Two and in *Meadows of Gold*, however, the picture is more complicated. Commentators have homed in on the meeting between the two authors, which they have placed in the years soon after Abū Zayd's move to Basra in 303/915–16; the meeting, in Miquel's analysis, enabled Abū Zayd to pass on to al-Masʿūdī the information contained in the full and finished *Accounts*.[38] This looks at first like a reasonable assumption, and it would, if correct, give a rough date of the early 310s/920s for the compilation of our Book Two. Certainly as regards the flow of information, it appears to be from Abū Zayd to al-Masʿūdī: the latter's language is the more polished, his organization of the material much better planned; Abū Zayd's work is the raw original from which he has drawn.[39] The only snag is that in the case of one *khabar*, the macabre story of an Indian who cuts pieces off his own liver before burning himself to death, al-Masʿūdī states that he himself witnessed the scene in India in 304/916–17.[40] If we take al-Masʿūdī's bona fides as read, and if we accept that the details of the story are so bizarre and precise that it is unlikely that another witness would independently have given the story to Abū Zayd, then it seems possible that al-Masʿūdī himself is one of the anonymous informants of the *Accounts*.

To those two pending questions, concerning the date of Book Two and the identity of its patron or instigator, there are no firm answers to be drawn from all this, but there are some comments to be made:

1. The meeting between al-Masʿūdī and Abū Zayd, whenever it happened, does not provide a fixed terminal date for the *Accounts*. The final version of the book might have been put together at any time up until 332/943–44, the year in which al-Masʿūdī was writing his *Meadows of Gold*.
2. There seems to have been a two-way exchange of information between the two men at their face-to-face meeting. Ultimately, however, by far the greater flow of material was from Abū Zayd to al-Masʿūdī.
3. Al-Masʿūdī was a busy writer: *Meadows of Gold*, which runs to over 1,500 pages of Arabic in the edition I have, is the smallest of three compendious works that he wrote (the other two seem to be lost),[41] quite apart from at least one other single-volume book. He would probably have been more than happy

to make use of material amassed over the years by Abū Zayd, the patient and discriminating collector of *akhbār*.

4. Lastly—and this is no more than a hunch founded on circumstantial evidence—it might be that al-Masʿūdī himself is that shadowy figure who "commanded" Abū Zayd to check through and supplement Book One, thus providing more rough gems to be mined, cut, polished, and inserted into his own more finely wrought *Meadows of Gold*.

The Literary Legacy

Al-Masʿūdī was not the only writer to delve into the *Accounts*' rich lode of data. Other writers were to draw from it—either directly, via al-Masʿūdī, or via each other—for centuries to come. They include some celebrated names in Arabic geography: Ibn Khurradādhbih, who, as early as the third/ninth century, borrowed from Book One material on the maritime route east; in the fourth/tenth, Ibn al-Faqīh and Ibn Rustah; later on, al-Idrīsī and al-Qazwīnī; and, later still, the ninth/fifteenth-century Ibn al-Wardī.

For centuries, then, the *Accounts* was the mother lode of information on the further Orient. There are several reasons. First, after that catastrophic Chinese rebellion in the later third/ninth century, there was little direct contact between the Arab world and China until the time of the cosmopolitan Mongol dynasty, the Yuan, in the seventh/thirteenth and eighth/fourteenth centuries. In the meantime, concerning the subcontinent of India and the rest of the Indian Ocean world, the only other sources of information were either suspect or, in one case, so abstrusely detailed as to be off-putting.

At the head of the first category is al-Rāmhurmuzī's *Wonders of India* from about the year 390/1000, in which the yarning sailors are finally given their say. In fact, many useful matters of fact do lurk in its picturesque jungles of legend, but a process of fabulation had clearly set in that would reach its climax in the Sindbad tales. Alone in the second category is the work of the highly serious early-fifth/eleventh-century indologist al-Bīrūnī. Faced, however, by chapter headings loaded with Sanskrit terms, such as "An Explanation of the Terms 'Adhimāsa,' 'Ūnarātra,' and the 'Ahargaṇas,'"[42] geographical encyclopedists, such as Yāqūt and al-Qazwīnī, must have scratched their heads.

In contrast, the material of the *Accounts* is reliable, valuable, and accessible. For a true successor to those traveling merchants of information, the Arabic reading world would have to wait until Ibn Baṭṭūṭah in the eighth/fourteenth century. As Miquel has said, that curious, objective, and tolerant traveler is their true heir.[43]

The Legacy Endures

Today, the *Accounts* is not only a major repository of historical information; it also shows us what endures. Much of the book may be literally exotic, but it is also strangely familiar (or, perhaps, familiarly strange): the irrepressible Indianness of India, with its castes and saddhus and suttees; the industrious orderliness of China, whatever the period and the political complexion, punctuated by paroxysms of revolution. The *Accounts* reminds us how those ancient civilizations mark time by the *longue durée*; how, as Jan Morris has said, "a century . . . [is] an eternity by British standards, a flicker of the eye by Chinese."[44]

Perhaps above all, the *Accounts* shows us a world—at least an Old World—already interconnected. It is composed of meshing economies, in which, even if communications were slower, repercussions of events were no less profound. Because of a rebellion in China, not only does a Tang emperor lose his throne, but the ladies of Baghdad, a 12,000-kilometer journey away, lose their silks,[45] and the brokers and merchant skippers of equally distant Sīrāf—the men who make the cogs of the economy turn—lose their jobs.[46]

Shades, or foreshadowings, of subprime-mortgage default in the United States and real-estate agents fleeing distant Dubai.

A Note on the Translation

The Arabic of the *Accounts* is often compressed, especially in Book One. In a translation that aims for clarity and ease of reading, interpolations are needed. Many are of a minor nature, for example, conjunctions (in which Arabic tends to be poor) and clarifications of whom or what a pronoun refers to. Interpolations of greater substance have at times been necessary to help the text make sense. English versions of two short quotations from the Qur'ān are this translator's own.

The only other English version of the *Accounts* was published in London in 1733 as *Ancient Accounts of India and China by Two Mohammedan Travellers, Who Went to Those Parts in the Ninth Century*; the translator's name does not appear on the title page. It has been reprinted as recently as 1995, in New Delhi. This version was done, however, not from the Arabic but from a French translation of 1718 by Abbé Eusèbe Renaudot. Sauvaget judged Renaudot's version to be good for its period though marred by "too many errors in reading and interpretation."[47] Despite improvements on the translations of both Renaudot and Reinaud, a new French version published in 1922 by Ferrand was also deemed by Sauvaget to include erroneous readings and interpretations, particularly in the field of geography.[48] This is, therefore, the first new English translation of the *Accounts* in nearly three centuries and the first made directly from the Arabic.[49]

Notes to the Introduction

1 2.15.3.

2 2.19.1.

3 Pellat, *The Life and Works of Jāḥiẓ*, 172–73.

4 2.19.1.

5 2.1.1.

6 Cf. Sauvaget, *Relation de la Chine et de l'Inde*, xxiv–xxv n. 8.

7 Sauvaget, *Relation*, xix and n. 7.

8 1.3.2.

9 2.1.1.

10 2.15.1.

11 2.1.1.

12 Al-Masʿūdī, *Murūj al-dhahab wa-maʿādin al-jawhar*, 1:145.

13 2.2.1.

14 2.1.1

15 2.4.1.

16 1.10.11.

17 Al-Ṭabarī, quoted in Mackintosh-Smith, *Landfalls*, 170.

18 Quoted in Zhang, "Relations between China and the Arabs in Early Times," 93.

19 2.9.1.

20 Yule and Burnell, *Hobson-Jobson: The Anglo-Indian Dictionary*, s.v. "Monsoon."

21 2.2.1.

22 On excavations at Sīrāf, see Hourani, *Arab Seafaring in the Indian Ocean in Ancient and Early Medieval Times*, 140–41.

23 2.2.1.

24 2.2.2.

25 Adūnīs, *Al-Thābit wa-l-mutaḥawwil*, 4:269 n.12.

26 For example, «Go about the earth and look at how He [God] originated creation.» Q ʿAnkabūt 29:20.

27 Al-Masʿūdī, *Murūj*, 2:228–29.

28 Al-Masʿūdī, *Murūj*, 2:299.

29 2.9.1.

30 Cf. Sauvaget, *Relation*, xxi.

31 E.g., do Indian kings pay their troops (1.7.2), or not (1.10.8)?

32 2.10.2.

33 Miquel (*Géographie humaine du monde musulman*, 1:121) used a different metaphor, of Islam as the watermark running through the pages of the book, "*l'Islam y est toujours vu en filigrane.*" That does not seem to give it enough prominence.

34 2.9.6.

35 2.4.3.

36 2.4.2.

37 Moseley, *The Travels of Sir John Mandeville*, 107–8.

38 Miquel, *Géographie*, 1:121–22 n. 4.

39 Occasionally, there are additional details of substance in al-Masʿūdī's renderings of information in the *Accounts*, such as the term *balānjarī* applied to the suicidal courtiers in India (*Murūj*, 1:211), and the number of Turkic troops fighting against Huang Chao, said to be 400,000 (*Murūj*, 1:139).

40 Al-Masʿūdī, *Murūj*, 1:210–11. Cf. 2.10.1.

41 Al-Masʿūdī, *Murūj*, 1:7–8.

42 Al-Bīrūnī, *Albêrûnî's India*, 424.

43 Miquel, *Géographie*, 1:126.

44 Morris, *Hong Kong*, 230.

45 2.2.1.

46 2.2.3.

47 Sauvaget, *Relation*, xvii.

48 Sauvaget, *Relation*, xvii.

49 Some of the material on India also appears in English in the first volume of H. M. Elliot and J. Dowson's *The History of India as Told by its Own Historians*, pp. 3–11.

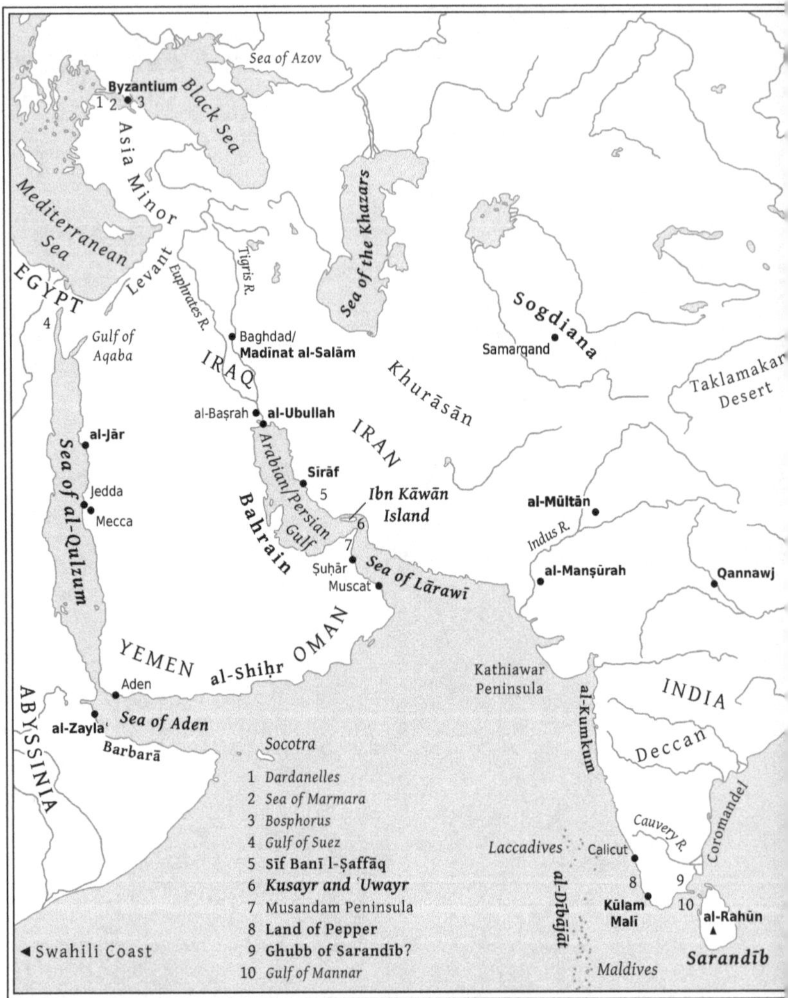

The Lands and Seas of Abū Zayd's *Accounts*

Muscat	Settlement/locality	OMAN	Land/country	*Maldives*	Island
		Levant	Region/landscape	*Black Sea*	Sea/lake

Obsolete or archaic forms of toponyms, found in the text, are shown in bold (e.g. **al-Jār**).
Place names with tentative locations are followed by a question mark (e.g. ***Maljān***?).

0 200 400 600 800 1000 km

Design: Tim Mackintosh-Smith
Cartography: Martin Grosch

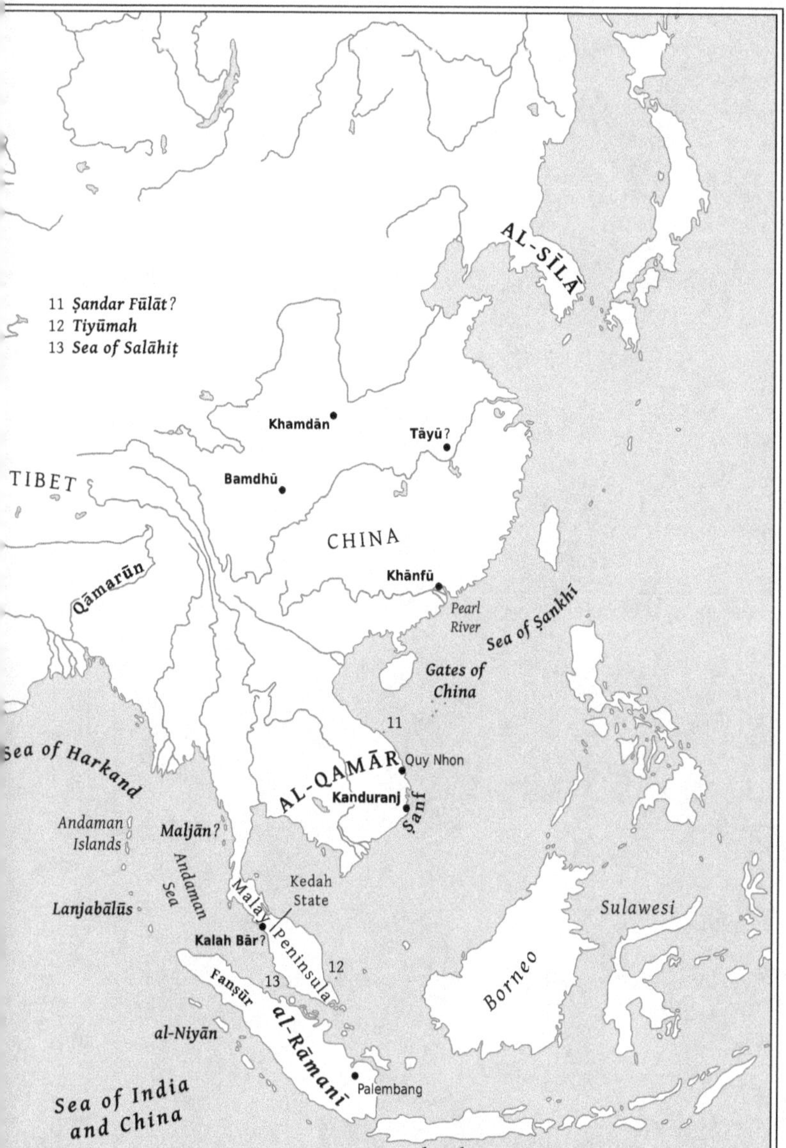
11 Ṣandar Fūlāt?
12 Tiyūmah
13 Sea of Salāhiṭ
AL-SĪLĀ
Khamdān
Tāyū?
TIBET
Bamdhū
CHINA
Qāmarūn
Khānfū
Pearl River
Sea of Ṣankhī
Gates of China
11
Sea of Harkand
AL-QAMĀR
Quy Nhon
Kanduranj
Ṣanf
Andaman Islands
Maljān?
Andaman Sea
Kedah State
Malay Peninsula
Lanjabālūs
Sulawesi
Kalah Bār?
12
13
Fanṣūr
Borneo
al-Niyān
al-Rāmanī
Palembang
Sea of India and China
al-Zābaj

Accounts of China and India

Accounts of China and India: The First Book

. . . like a sail.[2] It often raises its head above the water, and then you can see what an enormous thing it is. It also often blows water from its mouth, and the water spouts up like a great lighthouse.[3] When the sea is calm and the fish shoal together, it gathers them in with its tail then opens its mouth, and the fish can be seen in its gullet, sinking down into its depths as if into a well.[4] The ships that sail this sea are wary of it, and at night the crews bang wooden clappers like those used by the Christians, for fear that one of them will blunder into their ship and capsize it.[5] 1.1.1

The Sea of Lārawī[1]

In this sea there is also a kind of fish that reaches twenty cubits in length.[6] We caught one of these and split open its belly. Inside it was another fish of the same genus. We took this second fish out then split its belly open too—and there inside it was yet another fish of the same type! All of them were alive and flapping about, and they all resembled each other in form. This great fish is called the *wāl.* Huge though it is, there is another fish called the *lashak,* about a cubit in length, and if the *wāl* fish becomes so excessively greedy as to endanger the survival of the other fish in the sea, this small *lashak* fish is sent to overcome it. This it does by entering the inner ear of the *wāl* and not letting go until it has caused the *wāl*'s death. The *lashak* also attaches itself to ships, so the great fish do not go near ships, for fear of these smaller fish. 1.1.2

1.1.3 In this sea there is also a kind of fish whose face resembles that of a human and that flies over the water. The name of these fish is *mīj*. Another kind of fish watches out for it from beneath the surface of the water, and when the *mīj* falls back into the water, this second fish swallows it. It is called *ʿanqatūs*. All fish eat each other.

The Sea of Harkand

1.2.1 The third sea is the Sea of Harkand. Between it and the Sea of Lārawī there are many islands. They are said to be 1900 in number, and they are the boundary between these two seas, of Lārawī and Harkand. These islands are ruled by a woman. Ambergris of enormous size is washed up on the shores of these islands, and a single piece of it can be as big as a room, or thereabouts. This ambergris grows on the seabed as a plant does, and if the sea becomes rough, it is cast up from the bottom as if it were mushrooms or truffles.[7] These islands that the woman rules are planted with coconut palms. The distance between one island and the next is two, three, or four *farsakh*s, and all of them are inhabited and planted with coconuts. They use cowries for money, and their queen stores them up in her treasuries. It is said that there are no people more skilled in manufacturing than the people of this island group and that they can even produce a finished shirt on the loom, woven complete with sleeves, gores, and a placket at the neck. In their construction of ships and houses, too, as in all their other work, they reach the same level of technical perfection. The cowries, which have an animal spirit,[8] come to them on the surface of the water. A coconut-palm frond is used to collect them: it is placed on the surface of the water, and the cowries attach themselves to it. They call them *kabtaj*.

The islands of al-Dībājāt and Sarandīb

1.2.2 The last of these islands is Sarandīb, in the Sea of Harkand. It is the chief of all these islands, which they call al-Dībājāt. At Sarandīb is the place where they dive for pearls.[9] The sea entirely surrounds the island.[10] In the territory of Sarandīb is a mountain called al-Rahūn. It is on this that Adam descended, eternal peace be upon him, and his footprint is on the bare rock of the summit of this mountain, impressed in the stone. There is only one footprint at the summit of this mountain, but it is said that Adam, eternal peace be upon him, took another step into the sea. It is said, too, that the footprint on the summit of this mountain is about seventy cubits long.[11] Around this mountain lies the area where gems are mined—rubies, yellow sapphires, and blue sapphires. In this island there are two kings.[12] It is a large and extensive island in which aloewood,[13] gold, and gems are to be found, while in the sea surrounding it there are pearls and chanks, which are those trumpets that are blown and which they keep in their treasuries.[14]

Crossing this sea to Sarandīb, one finds islands that, although not many, are so great in extent that their exact size is unknown. One of them is an island called al-Rāmanī. It is ruled by several kings, and its extent is said to be eight hundred or nine hundred *farsakh*s. It has places where gold is mined and, in an area known as Fanṣūr, sources from which the high-grade sort of camphor comes.[15] 1.2.3

The islands of the Sea of Harkand

These large islands have other smaller islands in their vicinity. One of these is an island called al-Niyān, whose inhabitants have much gold. They live on coconuts, also using them as a condiment and as the source of an oil to apply to their skin. If one of them wishes to marry, he is only allowed to do so in return for a skull taken from one of their enemies. If he kills two of the enemy, he marries two women. Similarly, if he kills fifty, he marries fifty woman in return for the fifty skulls. The reason for this is that they have so many enemies that the more of them a man dares to kill, the more desirable they find him. In this island—I mean al-Rāmanī—there are many elephants, and also sapan wood and rattans.[16] There is also a tribe who eat people. The island faces two seas, those of Harkand and Salāhiṭ. 1.2.4

After al-Rāmanī lies a group of islands called Lanjabālūs. In them live a numerous people who are naked, both the men and the women, except that the women have the leaves of trees covering their pudenda. When the merchants' ships pass by, these people come out to them in boats both small and large to barter with the 1.2.5

crews, exchanging ambergris and coconuts for iron and such coverings as they need for their bodies, as it is neither hot nor cold in their land.[17]

Beyond these people are two islands separated by a sea that is called Andamān. Their inhabitants eat people alive. They are black and have frizzy hair,[18] hideous faces and eyes, and long feet—the foot of one of them is about a cubit long (meaning his penis)[19]—and they are naked. They have no boats, and if they did, they would eat anyone who passed by them.[20] It sometimes happens that ships make a slow passage and are delayed in their voyage because of unfavorable winds. As a result, the ships' water runs out, and their crews make for these people's islands to get water. When this happens, the islanders often catch some of the crew, although most of them get away.

1.2.6 After this island group, there are some rocky islets lying off the route the ships follow. It is said that there are silver mines in them. They are uninhabited, and not every ship that makes for them is able to find them. In fact they were only discovered when a ship passed one of the islets, which is called al-Khushnāmī, spotted it, and made for it. When day broke, the crew went ashore in a boat to gather firewood. They kindled a fire, and molten silver flowed from the ground, at which they realized that it was a source of the metal. They carried off with them as much as they wanted. When they set sail, however, the sea grew stormy, and they had to throw overboard all the silver they had taken. After this, people equipped expeditions to this islet but could not locate it. The sea is full of countless stories like this, of forbidden islands that the sailors cannot find, and of others that can never be reached.

1.2.7 *Dangers in the Sea of Harkand*

In this sea a white cloud may often be seen casting a shadow over the ships. From it a long thin tongue of vapor emerges and descends until it meets the water of the sea, at which the water boils up like a whirlwind. If this whirlwind makes contact with a ship, it swallows it up. Then the cloud rises, and from it falls rain containing debris from the sea. I do not know if the cloud draws up water from the sea, or how this happens.[21]

In each of these seas there is a wind that blows up and stirs the water, whipping it up until it seethes like cauldrons on the boil. When this happens, it casts up what it contains on to the islands that are in it, wrecking ships and casting ashore huge great dead fish. At times it even casts up boulders and entire outcrops of rock, as if they were arrows shot from a bow.

The Sea of Harkand, however, has another wind that blows from a bearing between the west and the Big Dipper.[22] This makes the sea seethe like boiling cauldrons and causes it to cast up large quantities of ambergris. The deeper the sea and the lower its bottom lies, the better the ambergris is in quality. And when the waves of this sea—I mean Harkand—grow big, the water seems to you like a blazing fire.[23] In this sea there is a fish called *lukham*, a predator that swallows people . . .[24]

Maritime Commerce between the Arabs and the Chinese

. . . in their hands . . .[25] so that the goods are in short supply. One of the reasons for such a shortage is the frequent outbreak of fire at Khānfū, the port of the China ships and entrepôt of Arab and Chinese trade, and the resulting destruction of goods in the conflagration. This is because their houses there are built of wood and split bamboo. Another reason for shortages is that outbound or returning ships might be wrecked, or their crews might be plundered or forced to put in to some place en route for long periods and thus end up selling their goods somewhere other than in Arab lands.[26] It can happen too that the wind forces them to land in Yemen or elsewhere, and they end up selling their goods there. They might also have to put in somewhere for a long time to repair their ships, or for some other reason. **1.3.1** *The Chinese port of Khānfū*

Sulaymān the Merchant reported that, in Khānfū, the meeting place of the merchants, there was a Muslim man appointed by the ruler of China to settle cases arising between the Muslims who go to that region, and that the Chinese king would not have it otherwise. **1.3.2**

At the time of the ʿĪds, this man would lead the Muslims in prayer, deliver the sermon, and pray for the sultan of the Muslims.[27] The Iraqi merchants, Sulaymān added, never dispute any of the judgments issued by the holder of this office, and they all agree that he acts justly, in accordance with the Book of God, mighty and glorious is He, and with the laws of Islam.

1.3.3 *Sīrāf in the Arabian/Persian Gulf*

Regarding the ports where the merchants regularly go ashore, they have said that most of the China ships[28] take their cargoes on board at Sīrāf. Goods are carried from Basra, Oman, and elsewhere to Sīrāf and loaded there onto the China ships. The reason for this is that, at the other ports on this sea,[29] the water is often too rough and too shallow for the bigger vessels to put in.

The Sea Route from Sīrāf to Khānfū

1.4.1 *From Basra to Muscat via Sīrāf*

The sailing distance from Basra to Sīrāf is 120 *farsakh*s. Once the goods have been loaded at Sīrāf, they take on board freshwater there, then they "take off"[30] (an expression used by seamen meaning "set sail") for a place called Muscat. This is at the end of the territory of Oman, the distance there from Sīrāf being about two hundred *farsakh*s. At the eastern end of this sea, the territories between Sīrāf and Muscat include Sīf Banī l-Ṣaffāq and the Island of Ibn Kāwān. Also in this sea are the rocks of Oman.[31] Among them is the place called "the Whirlpool," which is a narrow channel between two rocks through which small ships can pass but not the China ships.[32] Among the rocks of Oman are also the two rocks known as Kusayr and ʿUwayr, of which only small parts appear above the surface of the water. When we have passed all these rocks we reach a place called Ṣuḥār of Oman. Then we take on board freshwater at Muscat, from a well that is there. There are also sheep and goats in plenty for sale, from the land of Oman.

1.4.2 *From Muscat to Kūlam Malī*

From Muscat the ships set sail for the land of India, making for Kūlam Malī. The distance from Muscat to Kūlam Malī is a month, if the wind is constant.[33] At Kūlam Malī there is a guard post belonging to that country that exacts customs duty from the China ships, and there is also freshwater to be had from wells. The sum taken from the China ships is a thousand dirhams, and from other ships it ranges from ten dinars down to one dinar. The distance between Muscat and Kūlam Malī and the start of the Sea of Harkand is about a month. In Kūlam Malī they take on freshwater.

1.4.3 *From Kūlam Malī to Lanjabālūs*

Next, the ships "take off"—that is, they set sail—into the Sea of Harkand. When they have crossed it, they reach a place called Lanjabālūs. Its inhabitants do not understand the language of the Arabs or any other language known to the merchants. They are a people who wear no clothes and who have pale skins and sparse beards. The merchants have reported that they have never seen any of the women of this people. This is because it is their men alone who come out from the island in canoes, each hewn out of a single piece of wood, bringing with them coconuts, sugar cane, bananas, and coconut-palm drink. This last product is a whitish-coloured juice, which, if it is drunk as soon as it is tapped from the coconut palm, is as sweet as honey. If it is left for a while, however, it turns into an alcoholic drink; if this is then kept for a few days, it turns into vinegar.[34] All these products they sell in exchange for iron. They often find small amounts of ambergris, and this they also sell for pieces of iron. Their deals are struck entirely by gestures, and payment is made on the spot,[35] as they do not understand the language of the merchants. They are expert swimmers, and they often swim out and carry off the merchants' iron and give them nothing in exchange for it.

1.4.4 *From Lanjabālūs to Kanduranj*

Then the ships set sail for a place called Kalah Bār. Both "kingdom" and "coast" are called *bār*. It is subject to the kingdom of al-Zābaj, which one reaches by veering southward from the land of India. All the people of these regions of Kalah Bār and al-Zābaj are under one king. The dress of the inhabitants consists of waist wrappers,[36] and both their nobles and their lower-class people wear a single wrapper. The crews take on freshwater there from sweet wells, and they prefer the wellwater to springwater and rainwater. The distance to Kalah Bār from Kūlam, which is near the Sea of Harkand, is one month.

Then the ships go on to a place called Tiyūmah, where there is freshwater for anyone wanting it. The distance there from Kalah Bār is ten days. Next, the ships set sail for a place called Kanduranj, ten days distant. There freshwater is to be had by anyone wanting it, and this is the case for all the islands of the Indies—whenever wells are dug, sweet water is found in them. Here at Kanduranj is a mountain overlooking the sea, where fugitive slaves and thieves are often to be found.

1.4.5 *From Kanduranj to Khānfū*

Then the ships go on to a place called Ṣanf, a voyage of ten days. There is freshwater there, and from it the Ṣanfī aloewood is exported. It has a king, and the inhabitants are a brown-skinned people, each of whom wears two waist wrappers. When they have taken on freshwater there, they set sail for a place called Ṣandar Fūlāt, which is an island out to sea. The distance there is ten days, and freshwater is also to be had there. Next, the ships set sail into a sea called Ṣankhī, then on to the Gates of China. These are islets in the sea, with channels between them through which the ships pass.

And if God grants a safe passage from Ṣandar Fūlāt, the ships set sail from there to China and reach it in a month, the islets through which the ships must pass being a seven-day voyage from Ṣandar Fūlāt. Once the ships have gone through the Gates and then entered the mouth of the river,[37] they proceed to take on freshwater at the place in the land of China where they anchor, called Khānfū, which is a city. Everywhere in China there is sweet water, from freshwater rivers and valleys, and there are guard posts and markets in every region.

On Tides, and Unusual Phenomena of the Seas

1.5.1 In these seas the tide rises and falls twice a day. In the waters stretching from Basra to Banū Kāwān Island, however, high tide occurs when the moon is at its height, in the middle of the heavens, and low tide occurs when the moon rises or falls. Conversely, in the seas extending from near Ibn Kāwān Island to the region of China, high tide coincides with the rising of the moon, and low tide occurs when the moon is in the middle of the heavens: when the moon falls the sea rises, and when it returns to a point level with the middle of the heavens, the tide goes out.

Informants have reported that there is an island called Maljān, lying between Sarandīb and Kalah—in the Indies, that is, in the eastern part of the sea—in which there is a tribe of negroes who are naked and who, if they find anyone from outside their land, hang him upside down, cut him into pieces, and devour him raw. These people are many, and they inhabit a single island and have no ruler. They live on fish, bananas, coconuts, and sugarcane, and in their land are places resembling swamps and thickets. 1.5.2

They have also reported that in a certain part of the sea there are small flying fish that fly over the surface of the water, called "water locusts,"[38] and that elsewhere in the sea there are fish that come out of the water, climb the coconut palms, drink the sap of the palms, and then return to the water.[39] They have reported, too, that there is a creature in the sea resembling a crab that turns to stone if it leaves the water; a certain informant said that from this creature an ointment is extracted and used to treat various eye complaints. They have also reported that in the vicinity of al-Zābaj is a rocky island named "the Mount of Fire," near which it is impossible to sail. In the daytime smoke appears from it and at night blazing fire. At its base, cold freshwater comes out of one spring and hot freshwater from another. 1.5.3

The Chinese and Some of Their Customs

The Chinese, whether young or old, wear silk in both winter and summer. Their ruling classes wear the finest silk; other classes wear whatever quality they can afford. In winter, the men wear two pairs of trousers, or three, four, five, or even more pairs, according to what they can afford. This they do in order to keep the lower parts of their bodies warm, on account of the prevalence of damp and their fear of its ill effects. In summer they wear a single gown of silk, or something of that sort. They do not wear turbans. 1.6.1

1.6.2 Their staple food is rice. They often cook a sauce to go with it, which they pour on the rice before eating it. Their ruling classes, however, eat wheat bread and the flesh of all sorts of animals, including pigs and other such creatures. They have various kinds of fruit—apples, peaches, citrons, pomegranates, quinces, pears, bananas, sugarcane, watermelons, figs, grapes, serpent melons, cucumbers, jujubes, walnuts, almonds, hazelnuts, pistachioes, plums, apricots, serviceberries, and coconuts. Not many date palms are to be found in China, except for the occasional specimen in the garden of a private house. Their drink is a wine made from rice. Grape wine is not to be found in their land, and it is never imported—indeed, they do not know of it and do not drink it. From rice they manufacture vinegar, wine, jellied sweetmeats, and other such products.

1.6.3 The Chinese are unhygienic, and they do not wash their backsides with water after defecating but merely wipe themselves with Chinese paper. They eat carrion and other similar things, just as the Magians do; in fact, their religion resembles that of the Magians. Their womenfolk leave their heads uncovered but put combs in their hair, a single woman often wearing twenty combs of ivory and other such materials. Their menfolk, however, cover their heads with something like a cap. In dealing with thieves, their practice is to put them to death if they are caught.

Accounts of the Lands of India and China and of Their Rulers

1.7.1 *The four great kings of the world*

The Indians and Chinese are all of the opinion that, of the world's kings, four are to be counted as great. They consider the first of these four to be the king of the Arabs: it is a unanimous opinion among them, about which there is no disagreement, that of the four kings he is the mightiest, the richest in possessions, and the most resplendently fine in appearance, and that he is the king of the great religion to which nothing is superior. The king of China counts himself next in importance after the king of the Arabs, then comes the

Byzantine king, and finally Balharā, the king of those Indians who pierce their ears.

1.7.2 *Balharā and his kingdom*

This Balharā is the noblest of the Indians, all of whom acknowledge his nobility. Although each one of the kings in India rules independently, they all acknowledge his superior rank, and when his envoys arrive at the courts of any of the other kings, they make obeisance to them as a mark of honor to Balharā. He is a king who distributes payments to his troops as the Arabs do, and he owns many horses and elephants and possesses great wealth. His coinage is in the form of dirhams called *ṭāṭirī* dirhams, which are one and a half times the weight of dirhams in the coinage of the Arab realm. The coins are dated by the year of each king's reign, counting from the end of his predecessor's reign; in contrast to the Arab practice of dating from the era of the Prophet, eternal peace be upon him, they take their dates from their individual kings. Their kings live long lives, and often one of them will reign for fifty years. The people of Balharā's kingdom assert that their rulers' lengthy reigns and long lives on the throne are due entirely to their fondness for the Arabs. None of the other rulers shows the Arabs such affection as does Balharā, and his people share his fondness for them. "Balharā" is the name given to each of these kings, as is the case with "Kisrā" and so on; it is not a personal name. Balharā's rule covers territories beginning with the coast of the Sea of Lārawī, a region called al-Kumkum, and continues overland as far as China. He is surrounded by other kings who make war on him, but he has the upper hand over them.

1.7.3 *The king of al-Jurz*

Another of the Indian rulers is one called the king of al-Jurz. He has a large army, and none of the other Indian princes has the like of his cavalry. He is the enemy of the Arabs, although he acknowledges the king of the Arabs to be the greatest of rulers. No other Indian is as hostile to Islam as he. He inhabits a peninsula, where his people have great wealth and numerous camels and other beasts. They buy and sell using unworked silver as currency, and it is said that they have mines of silver. Nowhere in the land of India is one safer from robbery than in their territory.

1.7.4 On one side of al-Jurz territory is that of the king of al-Ṭāqā, whose kingdom is small. The women of this land are fair-skinned and are the most beautiful women in India. He is a king who maintains peaceful relations with his neighbors, because his army is small. He shows the same fondness for the Arabs as does Balharā.

The king of al-Ṭāqā

1.7.5 The next kingdom is that of a king called Dahmā. The king of al-Jurz makes war on him, and he does not rank highly as a king.[40] Dahmā also makes war on Balharā as well as on the king of al-Jurz. This Dahmā's army is bigger than those of King Balharā and of the kings of al-Jurz and al-Ṭāqā, and it is said that, when he goes on campaign, he takes about fifty thousand elephants with him. Consequently he campaigns only in winter, because elephants cannot endure a lack of water; he is thus able to go to war only in the wintertime, when enough water is available. Other reports put the maximum number of his troops at about ten thousand to fifteen thousand. In his land, garments are made that have no equal elsewhere: they are so finely and beautifully woven that one of them can be drawn through a finger ring. They are made of cotton, and we have seen one of them. In Dahmā's territory cowries are used for payment, for they are the currency of the land, or, in other words, its money. His territory also produces gold, silver, aloewood, and *ṣamar* cloths, which are made into fly-whisks.

King Dahmā, and the rhinoceros

1.7.6 In Dahmā's land the "marked *bushān*" or rhinoceros is to be found. This animal has a single horn on the front of its forehead, and within this horn is a marking, a naturally-occurring figure depicting the likeness of a human being or some other form. The horn is black throughout, except for this white figure in its interior. This rhinoceros is, by nature, smaller than the elephant but tends to be the same dark color as the elephant.[41] It resembles the buffalo and is so strong that no other animal equals it in strength. It has no knee joints, either in its hind legs or its forelegs, its legs being formed in one piece from the feet to where they join the trunk. An elephant will run away in fear from a rhinoceros. The rhinoceros is a ruminant, like cattle and camels, and its flesh is permissible for Muslims;

we have eaten it. The rhinoceros is found in large numbers in this kingdom, living in thickets. In fact, it is present throughout India, but the horns of these animals of Dahmā's realm are of finer quality and often contain the figure of a man, a peacock, a fish, and other such images. The Chinese use them to make belts, and in China the price of such a belt can reach two or three thousand dinars or more, depending on the fineness of the figure.[42] All of this horn in the Chinese market is bought in Dahmā's land for cowries, which are the currency of the land.

1.7.7 *Other kingdoms*

After Dahmā there is a king whose territory lies inland, away from the sea, called the king of al-Kāshibīn. His people are pale-skinned, have pierced ears, and are good-looking. Their land includes both open plains and mountains.

After this kingdom, on the sea, comes the territory of a ruler called al-Qyrnj, a king who is poor but proud.[43] Much ambergris is washed up on his shores; his land produces elephants' tusks and a little pepper, but so little that it is eaten while still green.[44]

After al-Qyrnj come so many kings that God alone, blessed and exalted is He, knows their number. One of them rules al-Mūjah, a pale-skinned people whose dress resembles that of the Chinese. They have large amounts of musk, and in their land are white mountains unsurpassed in height. They make war on many kings in the surrounding territories. The musk to be found in their land is of the very highest quality.

1.7.8

Beyond them are the kings of al-Mābud, whose land contains many cities. Their territory extends as far as that of al-Mūjah, and their people are more numerous than al-Mūjah. The people of al-Mābud, however, resemble the Chinese more closely still; they even have eunuch slaves appointed to tax them, as do the Chinese.[45] Their country adjoins China, and they maintain peaceful relations with the Chinese ruler, although they are not under his control. Every year, al-Mābud sends envoys and gifts to the king of China; similarly, the king of China sends gifts to al-Mābud. Their land covers a wide area. When the envoys from al-Mābud enter Chinese territory they are kept under watch, as they are so many that the Chinese fear they will take over their land. Nothing lies between al-Mābud territory and China but mountains and passes.[46]

China, and the Customs of Its Inhabitants

1.8.1 *The cities of China* It is said that the king of China has more than two hundred major cities under his rule, each of which has its own "king" and eunuch chief of finance[47] as well as several lesser cities under its governance. Among their major cities is Khānfū, the port for shipping, which has twenty lesser cities under it.

1.8.2 *The jādam* A "city" is only designated as such if it has *jādam*s. A *jādam* is an instrument that is blown, like a trumpet but longer, and of such a girth that both hands are needed to grasp and encircle it. It is varnished with the substance used on Chinese lacquerware[48] and reaches three or four cubits in length, with one end narrow enough for a man to place in his mouth; its sound travels about a mile. Every city has four gates, and each is equipped with five *jādam*s which are blown at certain times of the night and the day. Each city is also equipped with ten kettledrums, which are beaten when the *jādam*s are sounded. The object of all this is to proclaim their obedience to the king; it also enables them to know the times of night and day. In addition, they have indicators to regulate the hours.[49]

1.8.3 *Currency and commerce in China* They use copper coins for their transactions, and, although their treasuries are like those of other rulers, no other ruler has copper as the sole currency of his land.[50] They do indeed possess gold, silver, pearls, brocades, and silks, and all in large quantities, but all those are regarded as items of commerce, while the copper coins alone are used as currency. Ivory, frankincense, and copper ingots are imported into China, as well as *dhabl* from the sea, which are the shells from turtles' backs, and the *bushān*, which we have already described, namely, the rhinoceros whose horns they make into belts. Among the many types of animal they use for transport, they do not possess Arab horses but have other breeds instead; they also have donkeys and many two-humped camels. They have a fine type of clay that is made into cups as delicate as glass: when held up to the light, any liquid in them can be seen through the body of the cup, even though it is of clay.[51]

As soon as the sea merchants put in to harbour, the Chinese take charge of their goods and transport them to warehouses, guaranteeing indemnity for up to six months, that is, until the last of the sea merchants arrives.[52] Then, three-tenths of the goods are taken in kind, as duty, and the remainder is returned to the merchants. Any goods that the ruler needs he also takes, but he gives the very highest price for them and pays immediately, so he does no harm to the merchants. Among the goods he buys is camphor, paying fifty *fakkūj*s for a maund,[53] the *fakkūj* being a thousand copper coins. The same camphor, if the ruler had not bought it, would be worth only half that price on the open market.

1.8.4 *Funerary customs of the Chinese*

When one of the Chinese dies, he is not buried until the anniversary of his death. In the intervening period, they place the body in a coffin and leave it in their house. They put quicklime on the corpse, which absorbs the fluids from it so that it remains uncorrupted; their rulers are embalmed in aloes[54] and camphor. They weep over their dead for three years; all who do not weep, whether women or men, are beaten with wooden staves, and they say to them, "Do you not grieve for your dead?"[55] Eventually the dead are buried in graves like the graves of the Arabs. Up until the time of burial, however, they keep on giving food to the dead person, for they maintain that he eats and drinks: they leave the food by the corpse at night, and when next morning they find none of it left, they say, "He has eaten it." They do not cease weeping over the corpse and giving it food as long as it remains in their house; indeed, they will impoverish themselves for the sake of their dead and will spend every last penny and sell every last plot of land and spend the proceeds to this end. In former times, when they interred a king, they used to bury with him his household possessions, such as robes and belts (their belts being worth large sums of money), but they have now abandoned the practice, because one of these royal dead was dug up and the accompanying goods looted.

1.8.5 *Literacy* The Chinese, whether poor or rich, young or old, all learn how to form letters and to write.

1.8.6 *Rulers and other holders of high office in China* The titles of their rulers depend on their rank and on the size of the cities they govern. In the case of a smaller city, its ruler is entitled *ṭūsanj*, the meaning of *ṭūsanj* being, "he set the affairs of the city straight." In the case of a major city like Khānfū, the title of its ruler is *dīfū*. The eunuch chief of finance is called the *ṭūqām*; their eunuchs come from their own people and are deliberately castrated. The chief justice is called *laqshī māmkūn*, and there are other titles of this sort that we cannot set down accurately.

No one is given the office of ruler if he is less than forty years old, for they say of someone of this age, "Experience has taught him."

When one of the lesser rulers sits for a public hearing in his city, he sits on a judgment seat in a large courtyard, with another seat placed before him, and written submissions concerning the legal proceedings of the populace are presented to him. Behind the ruler stands a man called a *līkhū*, and if the ruler makes a slip in any of his pronouncements and gets it wrong, this official rejects the decision. They give no consideration to anything a petitioner has to say unless it is set down in writing. Moreover, before a litigant enters the ruler's presence, his written submission is examined by a man who stands at the palace gate and looks over each person's document; if it contains an error, he rejects it. Consequently only a scribe well acquainted with legal lore will write anything to be submitted to the ruler. Furthermore, he has to write on the document, "Written by So-and-so, son of So-and-so," so that, if it does contain an error, the blame falls on the scribe, and he will be beaten with wooden staves. The ruler never sits in judgment until he has eaten and drunk, lest he judge wrongly. Each ruler's stipend comes from the public treasury of his city.

In contrast to these provincial rulers, the Great King is seen in public only every ten months, for he says, "If the people see me more often, they will look on me with less reverence. Successful rulership calls for a display of kingly pride: the common people have no idea of fairness in a ruler, so a haughty attitude should be adopted towards them in order to increase our importance in their eyes."

1.8.7 *Sources of state income*

Their landed property is not subject to a tax; instead, they them selves are taxed per capita of the male population, according to the authorities' estimation of individual circumstances. In the case of any Arab or other foreigner resident in the land, a tax is paid on his property in order to safeguard that property.

If the price of grain rises too high, the ruler releases stocks from his granaries and sells it at less than the market price, causing the inflation to end.

The income of the public treasury comes from the poll tax. I believe that the daily income of the public treasury in Khānfū is as much as fifty thousand dinars, even though it is not the greatest of their cities.

Among the country's minerals, the ruler has exclusive rights to salt. He also has the rights to a plant that they drink with hot water and that is sold in every city for large sums of money, called *sākh*. It is leafier than alfalfa and a little more aromatic, with a bitterness to it. To prepare it, water is boiled, then the leaves are sprinkled on it, and it serves them as an antidote to all ailments. The entire income of the public treasury consists of the poll tax and the receipts from salt and this plant.

1.8.8 *The darā bell and the investigation of grievances*

In every city there is something called the *darā*. This is a bell hanging over the head of the ruler of the city and connected to a cord stretching until it passes over the middle of the highway, for the use of all the common people; the distance between the ruler and the highway is about a *farsakh*. If the cord is moved, even slightly, the bell moves too. Anyone who has a complaint against injustice moves the cord, causing the bell to move over the ruler's head. The complainant is then permitted to enter the ruler's presence, so that he may deliver in person an account of his circumstances and set forth his grievance. This procedure is in use throughout the land.

1.8.9 *Permits for travel within China* Anyone wanting to travel from one part of China to another obtains two documents, one from the ruler and one from the eunuch chief of finance. The document from the ruler is a permit for the road, made out in the name of the traveler and those accompanying him, and stating his age and his companions' ages, and the tribe from which he comes: all persons in China, whether of its native population or of the Arabs or other foreigners, are required to declare their ancestral origin from some group with which they may be officially identified. The second document, from the eunuch, concerns the traveler's money and any goods he may have. The reason for this procedure is that there are guardposts on the road where they examine both documents, and, when a traveler arrives at one, they write, "So-and-so, son of So-and-so, of Such-and-such an origin, arrived at our guardpost on the nth day of the nth month of the nth year, accompanied by So-and-so." This is in order that none of the traveler's money or goods should go missing. Whenever anything actually is lost or a traveler dies, the manner in which this occurred will be known and his property returned to him or to his heirs.

1.8.10 *Their fairness in financial dealings and loans* The Chinese act fairly where financial dealings or debts are concerned.[56] If someone makes a loan to another person, he writes a document to the borrower, obliging him to repay; the borrower also writes a document to the lender, marking it with a mark between his two fingers, the middle and index fingers.[57] The two documents are then placed together and folded in on each other, and an inscription is written across both of them at the place where their edges join. Finally the documents are separated, and the recipient of the loan receives his copy and acknowledges his debt. Subsequently, if one of the parties should repudiate the other, he is told to produce his copy of the document. It may then happen that the debtor maintains that he does not have one, whereupon the creditor's copy (in the debtor's own handwriting and with his mark) can be presented as proof, even if the version written by the creditor is, in fact, lost. In such a case, a debtor who still repudiates his creditor will be told,

"Produce another document, then, stating that this sum is *not* owed by you. And if you cannot, and the creditor's claim which you have repudiated is shown to be beyond dispute, then you will be made to suffer twenty blows on the back with wooden staves, and to pay twenty thousand *fakkūj*s of copper coins." The *fakkūj* being one thousand copper coins, this fine would amount to around two thousand dinars,[58] while the twenty blows would be enough to kill him. No one in China would willingly bring that upon himself, for fear of ruining both his person and his property, and we have never seen anyone agree to undergo it. Consequently, they act fairly towards each other, with no one ever foregoing his right to be repaid and without recourse to witnesses or oaths in their financial dealings.

1.8.11

Their procedure in cases of bankruptcy

If a man incurs the loss of other people's capital and his creditors then have him imprisoned in the ruler's jail pending restitution of their money, an acknowledgement of the debt is first obtained from him. Then, if and when he has remained in jail for a month, the ruler has him brought out and has a public proclamation made over him: "This man, So-and-so, son of So-and-so, has incurred the loss of the capital of So-and-so, son of So-and-so!" And if it then transpires that he has any money deposited with anyone or owns real estate or slaves or anything else that would cover his debt, he is brought out at the end of every subsequent month and beaten a number of times on the buttocks with wooden staves. This is because he has been staying in the jail, eating and drinking at government expense, when in fact he does own property: thus he is beaten, and whether or not anyone acknowledges that the debtor owns property, he is beaten all the same. They say, "Have you nothing better to do than to take what rightfully belongs to others and make off with it?" And they also tell him, "You must have *some* means of finding what you owe those people." But if, in fact, he does have no way out of the situation, and if the ruler is convinced that he really does own nothing, then the creditors are summoned and paid what they are owed from the treasury of the Baghbūn (this is the Great King, but his title is "the Baghbūn," which means "the Son of Heaven";

we Arabic-speakers call him “the Maghbūn”). After this, another public proclamation is made: “Whosoever does business with this bankrupt will be put to death!” As a result, hardly anyone ever loses money in this way. Also, if it emerges that the debtor does indeed have money deposited with someone else, and the latter has not admitted to having it, then that person will be beaten to death with wooden staves. In this case, the owner of the money will not be told anything; his money will be seized and shared out among his creditors, and no one will be permitted to do business with him again.

1.8.12 *Government concern for public health and education*

They have a stone tablet set up, ten cubits tall, on which is written in engraved characters a list of remedies and diseases, each particular disease paired with its appropriate remedy. And if a sick person is poor, he is given the cost of his medicine from the public treasury.

They do not have to pay a tax on their land; a poll tax is levied instead, varying according to the amount of landed and other property that they own. When a male child is born to anyone, his name is registered with the ruler, and when he reaches the age of eighteen he has to pay the poll tax. If, however, he lives to the age of eighty, he no longer has to pay the tax; instead, he is given a pension from the public treasury, for they say, “When he was young he paid us a tax; now he is old we pay him a pension.” Also, every city has a school and a teacher to teach the poor how to write, and the children of the poor are fed from the public treasury.

1.8.13 *Appearance and dress of the Chinese*

Their women go bare-headed, revealing their hair, but their men cover their heads.

There is a village in the mountains in China called Tāyū where the people are short in stature. Every short person in China is said to come from there.

The Chinese are a fine-looking, tall people, with clear, pale complexions tinged with red. No people have blacker hair than they. Their women cut their hair.[59]

India, and Some of the Customs of Its People

Moving now to India, if a man accuses another of an offense for which the mandatory penalty is death, the accuser is asked, "Will you subject the person you have accused to ordeal by fire?" If he agrees to this, a piece of iron is first heated to such a high temperature that it becomes red-hot. The accused man is told to hold out his hand, palm up, and on it are placed seven leaves from a particular tree of theirs; the red-hot iron is then placed on his hand, on top of the leaves. Next, the accused has to walk up and down holding the iron, until he can bear it no longer and has to drop it. At this point, a leather bag is brought out: the man has to put his hand inside this, then the bag is sealed with the ruler's seal. When three days have passed, some unhusked rice is brought, and the accused man is told to husk it by rubbing it between his palms. If after this no mark is found on his hand, he is deemed to have got the better of his accuser, and he escapes execution. Moreover, his accuser is fined a maund of gold, which the ruler appropriates for himself. On some occasions, they heat water in an iron or copper cauldron until it boils so furiously that no one can go near it. An iron finger-ring is then dropped into the water, and the accused man is told to put his hand in and retrieve the ring. I have seen a man put his hand in and bring it out unharmed. In such a case, too, his accuser is fined a maund of gold. 1.9.1 *Ordeal by fire*

When a king of the land of Sarandīb dies, his corpse is paraded on a low-bedded cart, lying on its back with its head dangling off the rear of the cart, so that the hair drags up dust from the ground. And all the while a woman with a broom sweeps more dust on to the corpse's head and cries out, "O you people, behold your king! Only yesterday he reigned over you, and you obeyed his every word. See now to what he is come and the manner of his going from this world. For the angel of death has taken his soul. Henceforth, let life delude you never more!" These and other such words she declaims, and the obsequies continue for three days. Then a pyre of 1.9.2 *Customs in Sarandīb on the death of a king* sandalwood, camphor, and saffron is made ready, and the corpse is burned on it and the ashes scattered to the wind.[60] All the Indians burn their dead on pyres; Sarandīb, the last of the islands,[61] is part of the land of India. At times it also happens that, when a dead king is burned, his womenfolk enter the fire too and are burned alive along with him; but if they wish, they do not do so.

1.9.3 *Indian ascetics* There are some in India whose habit is to wander the jungles and hills, seldom mixing with other people. Sometimes they live on leaves and jungle fruits and insert iron rings into the heads of their penises to stop them having sexual intercourse with women. There are some among them who are naked and others who stand upright all day facing the sun, naked too but for a scrap of tiger or leopard skin.[62] I once saw one of these men, just as I have described; I went away and did not return until sixteen years later, and there I saw him, still in the same position. I was amazed at how his eyes had not melted from the heat of the sun.[63]

1.9.4 *Among the Indians, kingship and occupations are hereditary* In every kingdom in India, the ruling family belong to a single dynasty from which the royal title never passes to another house; they appoint crown princes.[64] The case is similar with scribes and physicians: they all belong to distinct family lines to which the particular occupation is restricted. The various kings in India do not owe allegiance to a single ruler; instead, each is master of his own country. Balharā, however, is regarded as India's "king of kings."[65] In contrast to the Indians, the Chinese do not appoint crown princes.

Chinese and Indian Customs Compared

1.10.1 *Entertainments, wine-drinking, and the execution of unjust rulers* The Chinese are fond of musical entertainments; the Indians, however, regard entertainments as shameful and never indulge in them. They do not drink intoxicating drink, either, nor do they consume vinegar, because it is produced from such drink. This is a case not of religious belief but of disapproval. They say, "A king who drinks is not a king at all," the reason being that, in most Indian states, they are surrounded by neighboring kings who make war on them, so they say, "How can someone run a kingdom properly if he is drunk?" Sometimes kings fight each other for the control of a state, but this happens infrequently: I have never seen anyone actually take another king's country by force, except in the case of a people neighboring the Land of Pepper.[66] And if a king does conquer another kingdom, he appoints some member of the defeated king's family to rule it as his puppet,[67] because the people of the kingdom will tolerate no other arrangement.

In China, when one of the rulers under the command of the Great King acts unjustly, as sometimes happens, they slay him and eat him. The Chinese eat the flesh of all who are killed by the sword.[68]

1.10.2 *Marriage and adultery*

Among the Chinese and Indians, when people wish to arrange a marriage they first invite each other to feasts, then they exchange gifts. After this, they make the news of the marriage public by beating cymbals and drums. Their gifts are in the form of money, and the amount depends on what the people concerned can pay. Throughout India, if a man brings a woman home as his wife and she then commits adultery, both she and the adulterer are put to death. If a man forces a woman to have illicit sex with him against her will, he alone is executed; but if he fornicates with her as a consenting partner, they are both put to death.

1.10.3 *Theft and sodomy*

In all of China and India the penalty for theft, however great or small, is death. In the case of the Indians, if a thief steals as little as a *fils* or upwards, a long stake is brought, its end is sharpened, and then the thief is impaled on it, backside first, until the point comes out of his gullet.[69]

The Chinese sodomize boys who are provided for that purpose and are of the same order as female temple prostitutes.[70]

1.10.4 *Various manners and customs*

The Chinese use wood to build their walls, while the Indians build in stone, gypsum plaster, brick, and mud; these materials are however sometimes used in China also. Neither the Chinese nor the Indians are users of carpets.[71]

Chinese and Indian men marry as many women as they like.

The staple food of the Indians is rice, while that of the Chinese is wheat and rice. The Indians do not eat wheat.[72]

Neither the Indians nor the Chinese are circumcised.

The Chinese worship idols, praying to them and beseeching them for favors, and they possess religious texts.

The Indians let their beards grow long, and I have often seen an Indian with a beard three cubits in length. Also, they do not clip their moustaches. In contrast, most Chinese men are beardless by nature, for the most part. When someone in India suffers a bereavement, he shaves his head and his beard.

The Indians, when they imprison someone or keep him in confinement in his house, deny him food and drink for seven days. They are often kept in confinement.

The Chinese have judges who decide civil cases of lesser importance than those heard by provincial governors. The Indians also have such judges.

Leopards, tigers, and wolves are to be found throughout China. There are no lions, however, in either of the two provinces.[73]

Those who "cut the road" are put to death.[74]

Both the Chinese and the Indians assert that their idols speak to them, when, in reality, it is their temple servants who speak to them.

Both the Chinese and the Indians kill animals they intend to eat by bludgeoning them on the head until they die, rather than by cutting their throats, as the Muslims do.

1.10.5 *Personal hygiene*

Neither the Indians nor the Chinese bathe themselves when in a state of ritual pollution,[75] and the Chinese use only paper, not water, to clean their backsides after defecating. The Indians, however, bathe daily before eating their morning meal. The Indians do not have sexual intercourse with their women when they are menstruating; indeed, they find them so offensive that they turn them out of the house. The Chinese, on the other hand, neither stop having sex when their women menstruate nor turn them out. The Indians use tooth sticks, and no one eats before he has cleaned his teeth with one, and washed himself; the Chinese, however, do not do this.

1.10.6 *The relative extent of the two countries, and the varieties of fruit grown in them*

India is greater in extent than China, several times so, and has a greater number of kings. China, though, is more densely inhabited and cultivated.[76] Neither the Chinese nor the Indians have date palms, although they cultivate all other kinds of tree, as well as some types of fruit not to be found in our lands. The Indians, however, do not have grapes, and they are not common in China. All other kinds of fruit are to be found in abundance, although pomegranates are more common in India than in China.

The Chinese have no native tradition of religious learning; in fact their religion came from India. They maintain that it was the Indians who introduced the idols to their land and that they, the Indians, were the original people of religion. In both lands, they believe in the transmigration of souls as a basic tenet, although they differ on the resulting details of dogma. 1.10.7

Religion and science

India is the land of medicine and of philosophers; the Chinese also have medical knowledge. Most of their medicine involves therapeutic burning.[77] In addition, they have a knowledge of astronomy and astrology, although this is more widespread in India.[78] I do not know of a single member of either race who is a Muslim, and Arabic is not spoken.

The Indians possess few horses; they are more common in China. The Chinese, however, do not possess elephants and do not let them remain in their land, as they regard them as ill-omened. 1.10.8

Horses and troops

The king of India has many troops, but they are not paid as regular soldiers; instead, he summons them to fight for king and country, and they go to war at their own expense and at no cost at all to the king.[79] In contrast, the Chinese give their troops regular pay, as the Arabs do.

China is a more salubrious and finer land than India. In most of the land of India there are no urban settlements, but everywhere you go in China they have a great walled city. Also, China is a healthier country, with fewer diseases and better air: the blind, the one-eyed, and the deformed are seldom seen there, although in India there are plenty of them. 1.10.9

Cities, diseases, and rivers

In both countries there are big rivers, some of them bigger than our rivers,[80] and both have plentiful rain. India, however, has many desert areas, while all of China is populated and cultivated.

1.10.10 *Chinese and Indian dress* The Chinese are better-looking than the Indians and more like the Arabs in their dress and in their choice of mounts; in fact, their style of clothing when they ride out in public is quite similar to that of the Arabs, for they wear long tunics and belts.[81] The Indians, however, wear two waist cloths and adorn themselves with bangles of gold and jewels, the men as well as the women.

1.10.11 *Lands beyond China* The inland regions beyond China include those of the Taghazghuz, who are a Turkic people, and those of the *khāqān* of Tubbat; these regions adjoin the land of the Turks. In the other direction, that of the ocean, are the islands of al-Sīlā. They are a pale-skinned people who exchange gifts with the ruler of China; they maintain that if they did not keep up this exchange, rain would cease to fall on their land. None of our circle of informants has ever made it there and brought back a reliable report. In the land of al-Sīlā there are white hawks.

Here ends the first book.[82]

Accounts of China and India: The Second Book

2.1.1 *Abū Zayd al-Sīrāfī's evaluation of the First Book*

Abū Zayd al-Ḥasan al-Sīrāfī said: I have examined this foregoing book (meaning the First Book), having been commanded to look carefully through it, and to verify the information I find in it about the affairs of the sea and about its kings and their various circumstances,[83] and to compare this information with other reports passed down about these kings, known to myself but not appearing in the book. I found the date of the book to be the year two hundred and thirty-seven [851–52]—a time when maritime business still ran on an even keel, on account of all the toing and froing overseas by merchants from Iraq. I also found that everything recounted in the First Book follows a truthful and veracious line. The only exception is the report about the food the Chinese offer to their dead and which, when they leave it by the corpse at night then find it gone in the morning, they allege the dead person has eaten. This tale had already reached our ears, but we did not know if it was true until someone we trusted as an informant arrived from those parts. When we asked him about the story, he dismissed it as untrue and added, "The allegation is just as baseless as that of the idolators who claim that their idols speak to them."

The Changed Situation in China, and the Cause of It

2.2.1 *The revolution of Huang Chao, and the Khānfū massacre*

Since that above-mentioned date, however, the situation has changed, in China in particular. Because of events that occurred there, the trading voyages to China were abandoned and the country itself was ruined, leaving all traces of its greatness gone and everything in utter disarray. I shall now explain what I have learned concerning the cause of this, God willing.

The reason for the deterioration of law and order in China, and for the end of the China trading voyages from Sīrāf, was an uprising led by a rebel from outside the ruling dynasty known as Huang Chao. At the outset of his career he had been involved in armed banditry and hooliganism, causing general mayhem and attracting a rabble of witless followers. In time, when his fighting capacity, the size of his forces, and his lust for power had grown strong enough, he marched on the great cities of China, among them Khānfū: this city is the destination of Arab merchants and lies a few days' journey from the sea on a great river where the water flows fresh. At first the citizens of Khānfū held out against him, but he subjected them to a long siege—this was in the year 264 [877–78]—until, at last, he took the city and put its people to the sword. Experts on Chinese affairs reported that the number of Muslims, Jews, Christians, and Zoroastrians massacred by him, quite apart from the native Chinese, was 120,000;[84] all of them had gone to settle in this city and become merchants there. The only reason the number of victims from these four communities happens to be known is that the Chinese had kept records of their numbers. Huang Chao also cut down all the trees in Khānfū, including all the mulberry trees; we single out mulberry trees for mention because the Chinese use their leaves as fodder for silkworms: owing to the destruction of the trees, the silkworms perished, and this, in turn, caused silk, in particular, to disappear from Arab lands.

2.2.2 *The progress and eventual defeat of the revolution*

After destroying Khānfū, Huang Chao marched on one city after another, laying waste to each. So powerless was the king of China to withstand him that the rebel eventually closed in on the royal capital, known as Khamdān;[85] the king fled it for the city of Bamdhū on the border of Tibetan territory, and set up his court there. The rebel's power, meanwhile, kept on growing from day to day. His whole aim and purpose was the destruction of cities and the slaughter of their inhabitants, for he did not belong to any royal lineage and therefore could not aspire to gain the throne itself.[86] Moreover, he took his destruction to such extremes that China has remained in chaos down to our own times.

For a time, the rebel's campaign went on unchecked. And then the king of China wrote to the king of the Taghazghuz—a people from the land of the Turks, to whom they are neighbors and kinsmen by marriage[87]—and sent envoys to him, asking him to free him from the curse of Huang Chao. In response, the king of the Taghazghuz dispatched one of his sons against the rebel at the head of a vast number of troops, and, after ceaseless fighting and many great battles, Huang Chao was eliminated. Some people claimed that he was killed, others that he died a natural death.[88]

2.2.3 *The breakup of China and the decline of its foreign trade*

The king of China then returned to his city known as Khamdān, only to find it left in ruins by Huang Chao and to find himself debilitated, his treasury depleted, and his captains, commanders, and capable officers all dead. As a consequence, all the provinces were taken over by warlords: they prevented the central government from gaining access to revenues and kept hold of all the wealth that was in their hands. Because of the weakness of his own hand, necessity compelled the king of China to accept their excuses; for their part, the warlords feigned obedience to the king and pronounced the customary formulae of allegiance[89] but without actually obeying him in the matter of revenues or in other areas in which provincial rulers had formerly carried out the royal will. Thus China went the way of the Persian emperors when Alexander killed Darius the Great and divided Persia up among factional rulers.[90] Moreover the warlords, acting neither with the king's blessing nor at his bidding, supported each other in their quest for further power:

when a stronger one besieged a weaker, he would conquer his territory, annihilate everything in it, and eat all the defeated warlord's people, cannibalism being permissible for them according to their legal code, for they trade in human flesh in their markets.[91]

On top of all this, they extended the hand of injustice against merchants coming to their land. And, in addition to the harm done to the merchants, Arab captains and shipowners began to be subjected to injustices and transgressions. The Chinese placed undue impositions on merchants, seized their property by force, and sanctioned practices in which the custom of former times would in no way have allowed them to engage. Because of this, God—exalted be His name—withdrew His blessings altogether from the Chinese, the sea itself became uncooperative,[92] and ruin befell the ships' masters and pilots of Sīrāf and Oman, as ordained, in the course of events, by God the Ruler, may His name be blessed.

Various Practices and Manufactures of the Chinese

2.3.1 *How criminals are put to death*

One aspect of judicial practice among the Chinese was mentioned in the First Book, but only that one, namely, that married men and women who commit adultery are put to death, as are thieves and murderers. The actual manner of execution is as follows. First, the hands of the man to be executed are firmly bound and pushed over his head, on to the back of his neck; then his right leg is forced through the space formed by his right arm, and his left leg through that formed by his left arm. This means that both his feet are now at his back, and his whole body is compressed and remains like a ball; there is no way he can free himself, and no need of anything to hold him in this position. When he is in this state, his neck becomes dislocated, the vertebrae of his spine are displaced from their supporting tissue, the joints of his hips are twisted the wrong way around, and all the parts of his frame are compressed into each other: thus his spirit becomes constricted, and if he is left in such a position for even a part of an hour, he will perish. If however he remains alive too long, he is then beaten with a particular wooden stave of theirs, a particular number of times, on the parts of his body where the blows will be fatal; the number of blows is never exceeded, but it is never less than enough to kill him. Then he is given over to those who will eat him.

2.3.2 *The Register of Harlots*

Among the Chinese are certain women who do not wish to be virtuously married but prefer a life of sexual promiscuity. The practice is for such a woman to go to the office of the chief of police and declare her renunciation of the married life[93] and that she wishes to be entered into the list of harlots and to request that she be subject to the conventions customary for those of her kind. They have a number of conventions with regard to women wishing to lead a promiscuous life. For example, she must record in writing her ancestral descent, her physical appearance,[94] and her place of residence. She is then entered officially in the Register of Harlots, and a cord is placed around her neck from which is suspended a copper tag impressed with the ruler's seal. She is also presented with a written authorization that attests her entry into the list of harlots and states that she must pay such-and-such an amount of copper cash each year to the public treasury;[95] it also states that anyone marrying her is to be put to death. Thereafter, she pays her dues annually, and no opprobrium attaches to her. The women of this class go out in the evenings, dressed in all manner of attire, and unveiled.[96] They go to wanton and licentious foreigners who have arrived in the land, and also to the Chinese themselves, spending the night with them and leaving the following morning. We praise God for the guidance by which He has purified us from such temptations!

2.3.3 *Chinese copper coinage*

Regarding their use of copper coins to transact business, the reason for it is that they look on people who use gold dinars and silver dirhams as mistaken. For they argue that, if a thief enters the house of one of the Arabs who use dinars and dirhams, it is quite possible for him to carry off on his back ten thousand dinars and the same quantity of silver, which would spell ruin for the owner of the money. If a thief enters the house of one of their people, however, he can carry off no more than ten thousand of the copper coins, which are worth only ten *mithqāls* of gold.[97] These coins are made of copper alloyed with a mixture of other metals. Each of them is the size of a *baghlī* dirham and has a hole at its center large enough to take the cord on which the coins are strung. The value of each thousand of these coins is a *mithqāl* of gold: a thousand are strung on the cord, with a knot tied after every hundredth coin. When anyone buys land or any sort of goods or even something as cheap as vegetables, he pays with these copper coins, according to the price of his purchase. They are to be found at Sīrāf and bear a legend in Chinese characters.[98]

2.3.4 *Their manner of saving their possessions in event of fire*

Turning to outbreaks of fire in China and the information reported in the First Book about buildings, the cities there are constructed, as stated, of wood and panels of woven bamboo, rather like the reed panels of our lands.[99] The structures are plastered with clay and with a substance peculiar to the Chinese, which they produce from hemp seeds and which turns milk-white: when walls are painted with this, it gleams with extraordinary brightness. The doorways of their houses have no thresholds, because their goods and treasures and all their possessions are kept in chests mounted on wheels, so they can be moved about. If fire breaks out, these chests and their contents can be pushed to safety, with no threshold to impede their swift exit.

2.3.5 *Eunuch slaves, provincial rulers, and their manner of riding in public*

On the subject of eunuch slaves, which was mentioned summarily in the First Book, they function as overseers of taxes and as door keepers of the treasury. Some of them are of non-Chinese origin, captured in the borderlands, then castrated; others come from the native Chinese population and are castrated by their fathers, then presented by them to the ruler as a means of gaining favor. All matters to do with the ruler's own household and his treasuries, as well as with foreigners arriving in the city of Khānfū (to which the Arab merchants go), all this is the concern of these slaves.

It is a custom of theirs that when these slave officials and the rulers of all the various cities ride out in public, they are preceded by men with wooden instruments like clappers:[100] when they beat them, the sound can be heard from far away, and none of the populace remains on any part of the road along which the slave or the ruler intends to pass. Moreover, anyone who happens to be at the door of his house goes inside and shuts the door behind him until the slave, or the ruler in charge of the city, has passed by. Thus, not a single one of the common people is to be found along their route. The intention is both to impart a sense of fear and awe and to give the commoners no opportunity of gawping at their masters or daring to address them.

These slave officials of theirs, and their prominent military commanders, dress in silk of exquisite quality, the like of which is never exported to Arab lands because the Chinese themselves pay such inflated prices for it.[101] One of the prominent foreign merchants, a man whose reports are beyond doubt, related that he went to meet a eunuch official whom the Great King had sent to the city of Khānfū to take the pick of certain goods of Arab provenance that he needed. The merchant noticed that on the eunuch's chest was a mole, clearly visible through the silk garments he was wearing, and guessed that the eunuch was wearing a double layer of silk. When he realized that the merchant had been gazing so intently, the eunuch said to him, "I see that you cannot take your eyes off my chest. What is the reason?" The merchant replied, "Because I am amazed at how a mole can be visible through these garments of yours." At this, the eunuch laughed and held out the sleeve of his robe to the merchant: "Count how many I am wearing!" he said. The merchant did so, and found that he was wearing five tunics, one on top of the other; the mole could be seen through them all. Furthermore, the silk described here was of the raw, unbleached sort; the kind worn by their rulers is even more extraordinarily fine. 2.3.6

The diaphanous silks of China

Of all God's creation, the Chinese are among the most dexterous at engraving and manufacturing and at every kind of craft. Indeed, no one from any other nation has the edge on them in this respect. If a Chinese craftsman makes something with his own hands that he 2.3.7

The precise work of Chinese craftsmen

thinks no one else would be able to produce, he takes it to the gate of the ruler's palace, hoping that the excellence of his creation will gain him a reward. The ruler then issues instructions for the artefact to be displayed at the gate for a period of a year from the time of its receipt. If during this time no one finds fault with the piece, the ruler will reward its maker and enlist him as one of his recognized artisans; if however a fault is detected, the piece is discarded and the maker receives no reward.

It is said that a certain Chinese craftsman depicted, on a silk robe, an ear of corn with a bird perched on it, in so realistic a way that no one viewing it would have any doubt that it showed an ear of corn with a bird on it.[102] When the piece had been on display for some time, a hunchback passed by and found fault with it. He was admitted into the presence of the ruler of the city; the craftsman was present too. When asked what was wrong with the piece, the hunchback said, "Everyone knows that a bird cannot perch on an ear of corn without making it bend; but the depictor of this scene has shown the ear of corn standing straight up with no bend to it, and has then stuck the bird standing upright on top of it. That is his mistake." The hunchback was deemed to have spoken the truth, and the ruler gave the artisan no reward. Their aim in this and similar situations is to train the makers of such pieces, so that each one of them will feel compelled to guard carefully against faults and to consider critically what he makes with his own hands.

The Visit of Ibn Wahb al-Qurashī to the King of China

2.4.1 *Ibn Wahb admitted to the king's presence*

There was a man of Quraysh in Basra known as Ibn Wahb, a descendant of Habbār ibn al-Aswad. When the city was destroyed[103] he left it and ended up in Sīrāf, where he found a ship about to set sail for China. He was seized by a sudden desire that caused him, as was fated, to travel to China aboard the ship. On arrival he was again seized by a desire, this time to visit the Great King, so he made his way to Khamdān, traveling for about two months from the city known as Khānfū. He lodged by the palace gate for a long time, submitting written requests for an audience in which he stated that he belonged to the family of the Arabs' prophet. Eventually the king commanded that he be given accommodation in one of the official guest houses, and that any needs he lacked should be supplied. The king then wrote to his appointed governor residing in Khānfū, instructing him to make investigations and inquiries among the Arab merchants about Ibn Wahb's alleged kinship with the prophet of the Arabs, God bless him and keep him. When the governor of Khānfū wrote back confirming that this relationship was genuine, the Great King granted Ibn Wahb an audience and gave him a large amount of money, which he brought back to Iraq. This Ibn Wahb was a canny old man.

2.4.2 *How the Chinese classify world rulers*

Ibn Wahb informed us that, when he entered the king's presence, the king asked him about the Arabs and how they had brought about the end of the Persian empire. "With the help of God, exalted be His name," Ibn Wahb replied, "and because the Persians worshipped fire and bowed in prayer to the sun and the moon, instead of worshipping God." The king said to him, "The Arabs have indeed conquered the most magnificent of empires, with the most extensive lands for crops and grazing, the greatest wealth, the most intelligent men, and the furthest-flung renown." Then he asked Ibn Wahb, "How are all the kings ranked according to you Arabs?" Ibn Wahb replied, "I know nothing about them." Then the king said to his interpreter, "Tell him that we count five kings as great. The one with the most extensive realm is he who rules Iraq, for he is at the center of the world, and the other kings are ranged around him; we know him by the name 'the King of Kings.' Next comes this king of ours,[104] whom we know by the name 'the King of His People,' for no other king is more astute a ruler than we nor more in control of his realm than we are of ours, and no other populace is more obedient to its kings than ours; we are therefore the Kings of Our People. After us comes 'the King of Beasts,' who is our neighbor the king of the Turks,[105] and after the Turks comes the King of Elephants, that is, the king of India, whom we know as 'the King of Wisdom,' because wisdom originates with the Indians. Finally comes the king of Byzantium, whom we know as 'the King of Men,' for there are no other men on Earth who are more perfect in form than his men, nor any of more handsome countenance. These five are the foremost kings. All the rest are beneath them in rank."

2.4.3 *Portraits of the prophets*

Then the king said to his interpreter, "Say to him, 'Would you recognize your master if you saw him?'", meaning the Prophet of God, God bless him.[106] I replied, "How can I see him, when he is with God, glorious and mighty is He?" "I did not mean that," that king said. "I meant, if you saw his *picture*." To which Ibn Wahb replied that, yes, he would. The king then told them to fetch a certain casket, which was brought out and placed before him. From it he took a scroll, saying to his interpreter, "Show him his master." In the scroll I saw pictures of the prophets, and moved my lips in silent prayer for them.[107] The king had not imagined that I would recognize them, and said to the interpreter, "Ask him why he is moving his lips." He asked me, and I replied, "I am praying for blessings on the prophets." "And how come you can recognize them?" asked the king. "From the circumstances in which they are depicted," I said. "This is Noah in his Ark, saving himself and his people when God, exalted be His name, commanded the waters to inundate the entire Earth and all its inhabitants but preserved Noah and his people." At this the king laughed and said, "Noah you have named correctly. The inundation of the entire Earth, however, we do not acknowledge to be true. For the Flood only affected a part of the Earth; it did not reach either to our land or to India." At this point, Ibn Wahb commented: I was afraid to contradict the king and challenge this statement, as I knew that he would only dismiss my arguments.[108] He then resumed his account: Then I said, "And this is Moses with his staff, and the people of Israel," and the king replied, "So it is, although the land he occupied was a small one, and his people behaved wrongfully towards him." Then I said, "And this is Jesus, mounted on a donkey and accompanied by his disciples," and the king replied, "His time was short, for his career lasted only a little more than thirty months."[109]

Ibn Wahb went on to enumerate the circumstances depicted in the images of all the other prophets, but we have confined ourselves to mentioning only part of what he reported. He also maintained that he saw above each picture of a prophet a long inscription, which he supposed to include their names, the locations of their countries, and the causes of their prophethood. Then he said: I saw the picture of the Prophet Muḥammad, God bless him and keep him, mounted on a camel, with his Companions around him on their camels, with Arab sandals on their feet and tooth sticks stuck in their waistbands, and I wept. The king said to the interpreter, "Ask him why he is weeping." And I replied, "This is our prophet and our master and my cousin, eternal peace be upon him." The king said, "You are correct. He and his people gained possession of the most magnificent of kingdoms. But he never saw his possessions in person; only his successors saw them." Ibn Wahb added: I also saw pictures of other prophets, a great multitude of them: some were shown gesturing with their right hands, the tips of their thumbs and index fingers placed together, as if the gesture were a sign of truth; others were shown standing on their feet and gesturing with their fingers to heaven; and there were yet other poses. The interpreter maintained that all these were their own prophets and those of the Indians.[110]

2.4.4 *A dispute over the age of the world*

The king then questioned me about the caliphs, their appearance, and their mode of dress;[111] he also asked much about our laws and their various aspects, and I replied according to what I knew of them. Then he asked, "How old do you Arabs consider the world to be?" I replied, "The matter has been disputed: some have said six thousand years, some have said less than that, and some have said more, but only a little more." This made him laugh a lot, and his vizier too, who stood beside him, showing his disapproval of what I had said.[112] Eventually he said, "I do not suppose that your prophet said this," whereupon I blurted out,[113] "On the contrary, he *did* say that." However, I saw again the disapproval on his face. He then said to his interpreter, "Tell him, 'You must exercise discretion in what you say, for kings should be addressed only on the basis of properly acquired knowledge. You allege that you Arabs dispute this subject, whereas in fact you have only disputed what your prophet said. What is said by the prophets ought not to become a matter of dispute; rather, it should be accepted without question. Guard, therefore, against this and other such talk, lest you utter it again.'" And he said much else besides, but it was so long ago that it has slipped my memory.

2.4.5 *The generosity of the king of China to Ibn Wahb*

The king then said to me, "Why have you turned away from your own king, when he is so much closer to you than we are, both in abode and in blood?"[114] I replied, "Because of what befell Basra and because, when I arrived in Sīrāf, I saw a ship leaving for China. Also, because of what I had heard of the majesty of the king of China and of his bountiful goodness. All this made me long to travel to these parts and see them for myself. Now I shall return from here to my homeland, to the realm of my cousin, and I shall recount what I have witnessed of the majesty of this king and the extent of this country. I will have nothing but good to say, and I shall spare no fine word in my praise." He was delighted by this response, and commanded that I be given a right royal gift, and that I should then be conveyed by post mule to the city of Khānfū. He also wrote to the ruler of Khānfū, instructing him to bestow his own largesse upon me, to give me precedence over all the other rulers in his province, and to provide me with everything a guest could need until the time of my departure. As a result I lived in the greatest possible luxury and comfort until I departed from China.

2.4.6 *The city of Khamdān described*

We then questioned Ibn Wahb about the city of Khamdān, the seat of the king, and asked him to describe it. He told us of the city's extent and of its large population[115] and said that it was divided into two sectors separated by a long, broad street. The Great King, his vizier, his troops, the chief justice, the king's eunuchs, and all his relations dwell together in the right-hand sector, that is, on the eastern side. There is not a single member of the common populace to be found living among them, and no markets at all. The streets of this sector have streams flowing along them and are lined with trees planted regularly, and it has spacious residences.

In the left-hand sector, that is, on the western side, are to be found the general populace, the merchants, the provision stores, and the markets. At break of day you will see that the king's stewards and his relations, together with the palace slaves, and the slaves and agents of the army commanders, some mounted, some on foot, have all crossed over to the sector where the markets and the traders are. They get their daily allowances of provisions and whatever else they need, then they leave, and not one of them will return to this sector until the following morning.

Ibn Wahb added that in this city all kinds of delightful gardens and pleasant wooded glades can be found, with streams flowing through them. But there are no palm trees, for they do not exist there.

How the Seas Are Connected One to Another

Among the discoveries of this age of ours, unknown to our pre- 2.5.1
decessors, is the previously unsuspected fact that the ocean onto which the Sea of China and India opens is connected to the Mediterranean Sea.[116] This is something people would not have credited until our own time, in which news reached us of the discovery in the Mediterranean Sea of planks from the sewn ships of the Arabs.[117] These ships had broken up and their crews had been lost; the waves had pounded their hulls to pieces, and these were then driven by winds and currents which cast the planks into the Sea of the Khazars. From there, the timbers floated through the Gulf of al-Rūm, finally emerging into the Mediterranean Sea.[118] This points to the fact that the ocean turns north around China and al-Sīlā, continues around the back of the lands of the Turks and the Khazars, then debouches through the Gulf of al-Rūm, arriving at the Levant, the reason being that these sewn planks are used only for Indian Ocean

ships, and those of Sīrāf in particular. In contrast, the ships of the Levant and of Byzantium are nailed, rather than sewn, together.

News also reached us of ambergris being found in the Mediterranean Sea, a notion that would have been rejected, and indeed was unheard of, in past ages. For it would not be possible (assuming that the report is true) for the ambergris to have reached the Mediterranean Sea except via the Sea of Aden and al-Qulzum—this being the sea connected to the oceans in which ambergris is found—since God, exalted be His name, has placed a barrier between the two seas.[119] Instead, the ambergris (assuming again that the report is correct) must have been among the flotsam that the Indian Ocean cast into those other seas and that floated through them one after another, to arrive eventually in the Mediterranean Sea.

The Kingdom of al-Mihrāj

Account of the City of al-Zābaj

Islands in the kingdom of al-Mihrāj, and their products

2.6.1 Next we will begin an account of the city of al-Zābaj,[120] because it is situated opposite China; the sailing time between the two lands is a month, or less than that if the winds are favorable. The king of al-Zābaj is known as al-Mihrāj; it is said that its extent is nine hundred *farsakhs*,[121] although this king also rules over many other islands, and his entire realm is spread over a distance of a thousand *farsakhs* and more. His kingdom includes an island known as Sarbuzah, whose extent is reported to be four hundred *farsakhs*; also an island known as al-Rāmanī, extending to eight hundred *farsakhs*, which is home to the places where sapan wood, camphor, and other such trees grow. In addition, his kingdom includes the peninsula of Kalah, the halfway point between the lands of China and the land of the Arabs, whose extent is reported to be eighty *farsakhs*. At Kalah is the entrepôt for commodities such as aloewood in its different varieties, camphor, sandalwood, ivory, white lead,[122] ebony, sapan wood, aromatics of all sorts, and other goods that it would take far too long to detail. The trading voyages from Oman go, these days, as far as Kalah, then return from there to Oman.[123] The authority of al-Mihrāj is obeyed throughout these islands. His island of al-Zābaj, which is his seat, is fertile in the extreme and is settled and cultivated in a most orderly manner.

A trustworthy informant reported that, when the cocks of al-Zābaj crow at daybreak to announce the time as they do in our lands, they answer one another over a distance of a hundred *farsakhs* and more, relaying the call one to another, so continuous are the villages and so regularly dispersed. He reported, too, that there are no barren areas on the island, nor any signs of dilapidation. He also said that when anyone traveling around their land sets out on his mount, he goes as far as he pleases, but if he gets bored or his mount tires, he can break his journey wherever he wishes.[124]

2.6.2 *The Pool of the Kings, and the manner in which they hoarded gold*

One of the more extraordinary reports that has reached us from this island known as al-Zābaj tells of one of their kings—al-Mihrāj, that is—in days long past. His palace overlooked a *thalāj* leading to the sea, *thalāj* meaning the tidal reach of a river such as the Tigris of Madīnat al-Salām and Basra, which fills with seawater at high tide and through which freshwater trickles out when the tide is low. Connected to this was a small pool, immediately adjoining the royal palace. Every morning, the king's steward would bring an ingot of gold which he had caused to be cast, several maunds in weight (I was not told how many); as the king looked on, the steward would place the ingot in the pool. When the tide came in, the water covered this and the other ingots collected together with it, and submerged them; when the tide went out, the water seeped away and revealed the ingots; they would gleam there in the sunlight, and the king could watch over them when he took his seat in the hall overlooking them. He continued thus, his steward placing an ingot of gold in the pool every day for as long as that particular king lived, and not an ingot in the hoard would be touched. On the death of the king and subsequent kings, however, his successor would remove all the ingots, leaving not a single one. They would then be counted, melted down and shared out among the royal family, men, women, and children, as well as among their army commanders and slaves, each according to his rank and to the accepted practice for each class of recipients. Any gold left over afterwards would be distributed to the poor and needy. Finally, the number and weight of the gold ingots were recorded, so that it might said that So-and-so's reign had lasted for such-and-such a number of years and that he had left such-and-such a number of gold ingots in the Pool of the Kings and that they had been shared out after his death among the people of his kingdom. The longer a king reigned and the more ingots he left on his death, the greater his glory in the people's eyes.

The Land of al-Qamār and the Stupidity of Its King

2.7.1 *Description of the land of al-Qamār*

One of their accounts of the past concerns one of the kings of al-Qamār. This is the land from which Qamārī aloewood is exported; it is not an island, for it is situated on the continental landmass extending from the land of the Arabs. No other kingdom at all has a greater population than that of al-Qamār. They are men[125] who all regard adultery and all types of wine as prohibited, and nothing of this sort is to be found in their land and their kingdom. Al-Qamār is situated opposite the kingdom of al-Mihrāj and, to be precise, opposite the island known as al-Zābaj; the sailing time to cross the open sea between them is between ten and twenty days, given a moderate wind.

2.7.2 *The wish of the king of al-Qamār, and how al-Mihrāj heard of it*

It is said that the king in question ascended the throne of al-Qamār, in days long past, when he was still an impetuous youth.[126] One day he was sitting in his palace; this overlooked a flowing river of freshwater, like the Tigris of Iraq, and was a day's journey from the sea. His vizier was with him, and they had been speaking of the kingdom of al-Mihrāj—of how magnificent it was, and how densely populated and cultivated, and of how many islands were under al-Mihrāj's rule—when the king said to the vizier, "There is something I yearn for with all my soul and that I have been longing to see fulfilled." The vizier, a wise counselor who already had experience of the king's rashness, replied, "And what may that be, Your Majesty?" The king said, "I have been wanting to see the head of al-Mihrāj, the king of al-Zābaj, placed before me in a basin of brass." The vizier realized that it was envy that had stirred this idea in the king's soul, and he said, "Your Majesty, I would rather not have heard His Majesty saying such things to himself. For there is no current cause, either in deed or word, for any quarrel between us and those people, and they have done us no wrong. They are not neighbors to our land but live in an island far away from us, and they harbor no designs on our kingdom. It would therefore be inappropriate if these words of His Majesty's were communicated to any other person, nor should His Majesty mention the matter again."

The king, however, was enraged at this and would not listen to his counselor. Instead, he made his wish public knowledge among the commanders of his army and those of his most prominent companions at court. Tongues wagged, word spread, and it eventually reached the ears of al-Mihrāj himself. The latter was a man of sound judgement, swift action, and considerable experience, and had reached middle age. He summoned his own vizier and informed him of what he had heard, saying, "With all this talk circulating about that idiot and about that wish of his, inspired by his youth and recklessness—indeed, with his very words being repeated everywhere—we must not refrain from action. For if we did, it would weaken the strong arm of our rule and leave it diminished and enfeebled." He then instructed the vizier to keep what had passed between them secret but, at the same time, to make ready a thousand ships of middling size, all equipped for war, and to appoint an independent commander to each ship from among the arms-bearing men and brave warriors. The king, meanwhile, put it about that he intended to go on a pleasure cruise through the islands of his realm; he wrote to the local rulers in these islands, who were all loyal members of his circle, telling them of his decision to visit them and enjoy himself in their islands. Word duly spread of the intended tour, and the ruler of each island made preparations to give al-Mihrāj an appropriate reception.

2.7.3 *Al-Mihrāj's punishment of the king of al-Qamār*

When all was ready and in order, the king embarked with his fleet and sailed with it and his army across to the kingdom of al-Qamār. He and his companions are constant users of tooth sticks, every man cleaning his teeth with one several times a day; each man keeps his tooth stick with him and is never separated from it, or he keeps it with his slave.[127] The king of al-Qamār, meanwhile, had no inkling of what was happening, until, all of a sudden, al-Mihrāj burst into the river leading to the royal palace of al-Qamār. He landed his men, they surrounded the king of al-Qamār by surprise, and al-Mihrāj captured him and took over his palace. The king of al-Qamār's courtiers and officials fled before their master's eyes; al-Mihrāj, however, had it proclaimed that all would be under his protection. He then sat upon the throne[128] on which the captured king of al-Qamār had previously sat and had the captive and his vizier brought before him.

"Whatever drove you," he asked the king of al-Qamār, "to wish for something you were incapable of achieving, which would have brought you no good fortune even if you had attained it, and when there was nothing to make you set out on such a course in the first place?" To this the king of al-Qamār had no response. Al-Mihrāj continued, "Now, had you wished—along with your wish to see my head placed before you in a basin of brass—to make free with my land and take it over or to cause mischief in any part of it, then I would have done all that to *you*. But your wish was for something specific. So I shall now do this thing to you, then return to my country without laying hands on anything in your land, whether great or small. This is so you will be an example to warn those that come after you, so that no one should seek to exceed the bounds of his allotted abilities, and so that everyone should instead make the most of being free from such confusion."[129] Having said this, he had the head of the king of al-Qamār cut off.

Al-Mihrāj then turned to the executed king's vizier and said, "May God reward you for being so excellent a vizier. For I have ascertained that the advice you gave your master was sound—if only he had taken it. Consider now who will be fit to succeed that idiot as king, and install him in his place."

Al-Mihrāj then departed immediately on the voyage back to his country; neither he nor anyone from his force had laid hands on anything in the land of al-Qamār. When he arrived back in his kingdom, he sat upon his throne, surveyed his pool,[130] and had the basin of brass put before him in which the head of the king of al-Qamār had been placed. He then summoned the prominent men of his kingdom, told them the story of the head, and explained what had led him to undertake such a venture. On hearing this, the dignitaries of the realm prayed God to reward him for what he had done. The king then gave orders for the head to be washed and embalmed with perfumes; he had it placed in a casket, and sent it back to the new ruler who had succeeded the executed king on the throne of the land of al-Qamār. With it he wrote a letter: "I was induced to act as we did with your former master by his outrageous threat to us and by the need to punish such behavior in others; for we had been told of what he wished to do to us. We have decided, however, to restore his head to you, because keeping it locked up here would achieve no end and because the goal we have already gained through it can bring us no more glory." 2.7.4

The return home of al-Mihrāj

The news of al-Mihrāj's deed reached the kings of India and China, and his importance swelled in their eyes. And, ever after, when the kings of al-Qamār rose in the morning, they would stand and turn their faces towards the land of al-Zābaj, then bow and prostrate themselves to al-Mihrāj, out of reverence to him.

The Belief of the Eastern Kings in the Transmigration of Souls

All the kings of India and China believe in the transmigration of souls 2.8.1
and hold it as an article of faith. A trustworthy informant reported that one of their kings in these lands was afflicted by smallpox. When he had recovered, he looked in the mirror and thought how hideous his face had become.[131] Seeing one of his brother's sons, he

said to him, "It is not for the like of me to dwell in this body, now it is so changed. The body is, after all, a mere receptacle for the soul; when the soul passes out of it, it returns in another receptacle. You must be king in my place, for I shall now disjoin my soul from my body, until such time as I alight in another body." He then called for a dagger of his that had a particularly sharp edge, and commanded that his head be severed with it. He was duly decapitated, then his corpse was burned.

Accounts of China Continued

Various Matters Relating to the Chinese

2.9.1 *The concern of their kings for investigating merchants' complaints*

The Chinese used to monitor their own system—in the old days, that is, before its deterioration in the present time—with a rigor unheard of elsewhere. An example of this is the story of a certain man from Khurasan who came to Iraq, bought a large quantity of goods, and took them out to China. He was of a miserly and exceedingly avaricious nature, and a dispute arose between him and one of the Great King's eunuchs, who had been sent by his master to Khānfū (the city to which the Arab merchants go) to get various items the king required from among the goods imported on Arab ships; this eunuch was one of the king's most respected slaves and was in charge of the royal treasuries and other property. The dispute was over certain ivory and other goods, which the merchant held out against selling at the price offered until things reached a heated impasse, at which the eunuch took it upon himself to seize by force the pick of the merchant's goods, and treated him with contempt.

Following this, the Khurasani set out incognito and traveled to Khamdān, the Great King's capital, taking two months and more on the journey. On his arrival, he went to the chain attached to the bell that was described in the First Book.[132] Now, the procedure for anyone who pulls the chain to ring the bell hanging over the Great King is as follows. He is first removed to a place ten days' journey distant, by way of banishment, and ordered to be placed under detention there for two months. At the end of that period, the ruler of the province concerned brings him out of detention and says to him, "You have exposed yourself to the risk of your own perdition and the shedding of your blood, if it emerges that you have been lying. For the Great King has already given you and your like direct access to ministers and provincial rulers of his, through whom it is not difficult for you to obtain justice. You must be aware that, if you take your case to the Great King and it transpires that your complaint is not grave enough to entail an appeal to him, then the outcome will be nothing less than your death: this is to deter everyone else who might consider a similar course of action from daring to do what you have dared. Retract your complaint, therefore, so that we may release you; go back to your own business." If the complainant then withdraws his case, he is dealt fifty blows with a wooden stave and deported to his country of origin; if, however, he decides to pursue his complaint, he is admitted to the Great King's presence. This procedure was followed with the Khurasani; he persisted in his complaint and requested an audience.

He was thus duly dispatched and entered the king's presence. The interpreter questioned him about his case, and the Khurasani told him how the eunuch slave had mistreated him and had snatched his property out of his hands. Meanwhile, the affair of the Khurasani had already become public knowledge in Khānfū, and news of it had spread through the city. The king therefore ordered that the Khurasani be detained and supplied with all necessary food and drink; at the same time, he instructed his vizier to write to the government representatives in Khānfū, telling them to investigate the Khurasani's allegation and to ascertain the truth of the matter. He also ordered similar investigations to be undertaken by the commanders of the right and left wings of the army and the commander of the center; after the vizier, it is upon these three that control of the king's forces devolves: he trusts them with his life, and if he rides out with them to do battle or for some other purpose, each one of them rides with him, in rank. Eventually each one of these officers wrote independently to the Great King, having uncovered enough evidence about the matter to apprise himself of the truth of the Khurasani's allegation. Other similar reports on the case kept reaching the king from every quarter, and the eunuch was summoned. When he appeared, the king seized his property and deprived him of control over his own treasuries. He then said to him, "You deserve to be put to death. For you exposed me to the risk of losing face on account of a man who journeyed from Khurasan, on the border of my kingdom, and made his way to the land of the Arabs, and from there to the kingdoms of the Indians, and then came to my land, all in pursuit of honorable gain—and whom you then wanted to return by way of these same kingdoms, telling everyone in them, 'I was treated unjustly in China, and my property was seized by force'! But I am loath to shed your blood, if only because you have enjoyed my protection for so long. Instead, I shall appoint you to manage the dead, because you have failed in your management of the living." And the king commanded that the eunuch be given a position guarding and overseeing the royal cemeteries.

2.9.2 *The chief justice of China*

Another example of their admirable governance in the old days (but not in this time) was the status of the law and the high regard they had for it in their hearts. They would select someone to dispense the law only if they had no doubt in their minds about his knowledge of their legal code, the truth of his words, the correctness of his conduct in all his affairs, and his refusal to turn a blind eye to the misdeeds of those of high status—their intention being that right be done wherever it is due, and that their judges should have no designs on the property of the vulnerable or on any sums passing through their hands.

When they decide to appoint a chief justice, they send him, before his appointment, on a tour of all the cities that are the chief ones in their land. The object is for him to stay in each city for a month or two, looking into the affairs of its inhabitants, hearing their reports, and learning about their customary practices; also, it is so that he can get to know directly which citizens are trustworthy in what they say[133] and will thus not need to ask intermediaries.

When he has been taken around these provincial capitals and none of the great cities of the kingdom remains unvisited, he makes his way to the royal palace to be installed as chief justice; their selection of him is now confirmed, and he takes up their appointment. Moreover, he is now fully acquainted with the entire kingdom and with which of the citizens or others in each city should be appointed as provincial judges. This sort of personal knowledge saves him from having to seek advice on such appointments from those who, when questioned, may be biased or untruthful in their replies. Besides, none of his provincial judges will subsequently be prepared either to write reports to him containing anything contrary to the facts he knows, or to omit mention of such facts from their side.

Every day, the chief justice has a crier proclaim these words at his gate: "Does any of you have a complaint for the king who is veiled from his subjects' eyes, or against one of the king's relations or his commanders or any other of his subjects? For it is I who am deputed by him to deal with all such grievances, by virtue of the power he has placed in my hands and the office with which he has invested me!" He proclaims this three times. The reason is that, according to their understanding of the monarchy, the king will only be deposed when reports of flagrant injustice arrive from the offices of provincial rulers and when the king himself neglects the law and those who dispense it. Equally, they believe that, as long as the king guards against these two failings—with the result that official reports bring news only of just administration and that only those who act rightly are appointed to be judges—then the monarchy will maintain its proper harmony.[134]

2.9.3 *China's western borders and neighboring countries*

Regarding Khurasan and its proximity to the land of China, between the latter and Sogdiana there is a journey of two months. The way, however, is via a forbidding desert of unbroken sand dunes in which there are no water sources and no river valleys, with no habitation nearby.[135] This is what prevents the people of Khurasan from launching an assault on China. Turning to the part of China lying in the direction of the setting sun, namely the place known as

Bamdhū, this is located on the borders of Tibet, and fighting never ceases there between the Chinese and the Tibetans.

2.9.4 *Musk and its origin* We have seen one of the people who entered China, who reported that he saw a man carrying on his back a skin bag filled with Tibetan musk; this man had come on foot from Samarqand, passing through one Chinese city after another until he finally arrived in Khānfū, the meeting place of merchants coming from Sīrāf. This journey was possible because the land that is home to the gazelles that produce Chinese musk is one and the same land with Tibet: the Chinese catch the gazelles nearest to them, and the Tibetans those nearest to them.[136] Furthermore, the superiority of Tibetan musk to Chinese is due to only two factors. The first of these is the fact that musk gazelles in the Tibetan borderlands graze on Indian spikenard,[137] whereas those in the region neighboring China graze on other kinds of herbage. The second factor is the Tibetans' practice of leaving the musk pods in their natural state.[138] The Chinese, in contrast, adulterate the musk pods that they get hold of; there is the additional factor of their using the maritime route to export the musk and the exposure to moist vapors that this incurs. If the Chinese were to leave the musk intact in its pods and then place the pods in earthenware pots, sealing them securely, then their musk would be of the same quality as Tibetan musk when it reached Arab lands.[139]

The best musk of all in quality is that which the gazelle has rubbed onto stones in the mountains.[140] Musk is a substance that goes to the gazelle's navel and gathers there like uncoagulated blood, just as blood itself gathers in the superficial parts of boils. When the swollen pod "ripens," the gazelle rubs it against stones and chafes it until the musk starts to ooze out on to the stones; the gazelle eventually bursts it, and its contents flow out. When all the musk has come out, the pod dries up and scabs over, then the substance begins to gather in it as before. The Tibetans have men who go out in search of this musk deposited on stones and who have expert knowledge of it. When they find some, they pick it off the stone, gather it together, and pack it into empty musk pods; it is then taken to their kings. This is the very best musk of all, because it has ripened in its pods on the living animal. It is superior to other sorts of musk, in the same way that fruit ripened on the tree is superior to all other fruit that is picked before it is ripe.

Except for this kind, all musk is from gazelles that are trapped in enclosures of nets staked upright or hunted with arrows, and often the pods are cut out of the gazelle before the musk in them has ripened. Besides, when it is cut out of the gazelles, it retains an unpleasant odor for a certain time, until it dries, this taking a long period of days; as it dries out, its substance changes and turns into musk. The musk gazelle itself resembles the other types of gazelle found in our lands, both in size and color, and has similarly slender legs and cloven hoofs, and horns that rise straight and then curve in a similar way.[141] However, the musk gazelle has a pair of slender white tusks, one on each side of its lower jaw, standing up in front of its face; the length of each is about the distance between the tips of a man's thumb and index finger when stretched apart, or less than that, and its shape is that of an elephant's tusk in miniature.[142] This is the difference between the musk gazelle and other gazelles.

2.9.5 *Post mules*

The correspondence of the Great Kings of China with the rulers of their provincial capitals and with their eunuch officials goes on post mules. These have their tails clipped in the manner of our post mules[143] and follow recognized routes.

2.9.6 *The Chinese manner of urination*

Further to what we have already said in description of the rulers of the Chinese is the fact that they urinate from a standing position; so too do all those of their subjects who belong to the native population.[144] The rulers themselves, the army commanders and the other people of high rank use tubes of lacquered wood, each a cubit in length and with a hole at either end, the upper one big enough for the user to insert the head of his penis: when he wants to urinate, he stands on his feet, aims the tube away from himself, and urinates through it. They maintain that this method is healthier for their bodies, that the pain from bladder stones felt in the bladder itself and during urination is entirely due to the practice of squatting to urinate, and that the bladder allows its contents to well up and flow out only when one urinates standing.[145]

2.9.7 *The reason Chinese men let their hair grow*

The reason they let their hair grow on their heads—I mean the men—is the fact that they do not believe in "rounding" the heads of new-born babies and letting them harden, as is practiced by the Arabs.[146] They say that the practice is one of the causes of the brain becoming displaced from the position in which it was created and that it interferes with the normal faculties of sensation. As a result, their heads are covered in bumps, which their hair covers up and hides from view.

2.9.8 *Choice of spouses among the Chinese*

Regarding the choice of spouses in China, the Chinese are made up of different peoples and tribes (just as the Israelites and Arabs are peoples and subtribes) all recognizing one another among themselves.[147] None of the Chinese, however, is ever married to a near relation or to anyone sharing the same immediate lineage; indeed, they take this even further, to the extent that members of a particular tribe will never marry within that tribe. The Arab equivalent would be for members of Tamīm never to marry within Tamīm, and for Rabīʿah never to marry within Rabīʿah; instead, Rabīʿah would only marry spouses from Muḍar, and Muḍar from Rabīʿah. The Chinese claim that this produces better-developed offspring.

Further Accounts of India

2.10.1 *The Indians who burn themselves to death*

In the kingdom of Balharā and those of other Indian rulers, there are people who burn themselves to death with fire. This stems from their belief in the transmigration of souls, which has so firm a place in the hearts, and from their desire to banish from themselves any doubts about it.

Certain kings of theirs, when they ascend the throne, have rice cooked for them and placed before them on banana leaves. The new king invites three or four hundred of his companions—they come of their own free choice, not under any compulsion from the king—and gives them some of the rice, having first eaten some himself; one by one they come up to him, take a little of the rice, and eat it. It then becomes obligatory for all those who have eaten some of this rice, when the king dies or is killed, to burn themselves to death by fire. This they must do to the last man, and on the very day of the king's death, without delay, until not a single one of them remains, or even a trace of them.

If someone from the general populace makes up his mind to burn himself to death, he first goes to the gate of the king's palace to ask permission to do so, then he goes around in the markets. In the meantime a fire has been kindled for him in a huge great pile of firewood; there are men in charge of this who stoke the flames until they blaze red-hot, as red as carnelian. The man then begins to run around the markets, preceded by people clashing cymbals and surrounded by members of his family and close kin. One of these now places on his head a wreath made from aromatic plants, fills the space in the center of it with burning embers, and sprinkles them with sandarac, which has the same effect on fire as does naphtha.[148] The man walks on, the crown of his head ablaze and giving off the reek of burning flesh, but he does not alter his pace or show any fear, until at last he reaches the pyre, leaps into the flames, and is burned to ashes.

An informant who was present when one of these men was intending to enter the fire reported that, when he was on the point of doing so, the man took a dagger, placed the point of it at the top of his abdomen[149] and, with his own hand, ripped himself open down to below the navel. He plunged his left hand into his innards, grasped his own liver and pulled out as much as he could, speaking all the while, then sliced off a piece of the liver and handed it to his brother—all to demonstrate his contempt of death and his ability to bear pain—and finally launched himself into the flames and into God's damnation.

2.10.2 *Rival gangs among the Indians, and their extraordinary challenges to each other*

This same informant also maintained that, in the uplands of this region, live a group of Indians who, in their pursuit of the pointless and idiotic, resemble the Kanīfiyyah and the Jalīdiyyah in our lands, and that they and the coastal people are gang rivals. Men from the coast, the informant stated, continually go to the uplands and challenge the uplanders to match them in trials of endurance; similarly, the uplanders go and challenge the men of the coast. For example, an uplander went to the coastal people to issue such a challenge. A crowd gathered around him, some of them onlookers and some of them gang members. The uplander demanded that the gang members do what he was about to do; if they could not, they would have to admit defeat. The challenger then went and sat at the edge of some bamboo thickets and told the people to bend one of the bamboo stems downwards. Now, these bamboos are all tangled together like reeds, but their bases are as thick as large storage jars, or thicker;[150] if the top of a bamboo is pushed downwards, the stem will respond by bending nearly to the ground, and if it is let go, it will spring back to its upright position. So the top of a thick bamboo was duly bent down until it was by the man. He then tied his long plaited hair to the stem with a tight knot, took a dagger—theirs have blades that cut as swift as fire—and said to the onlookers, "I am going to cut off my head with this dagger. The moment it is separated from my body, let it go. And as soon as the bamboo has sprung back to its upright position, taking my head with it, I will laugh out loud, and you will hear a short burst of chuckling." The men of the coast were unable to emulate his act.[151] We have heard this account from someone we do not suspect of lying; indeed, the story is now common knowledge, because these regions of India are close to Arab lands, and such accounts reach the Arabs from there all the time.

2.10.3 *Voluntary euthanasia among the elderly*

It is a feature of the Indians, when old age saps the strength of their men and women and their faculties become impaired, that someone in this state will ask his family to put him alive on a pyre or drown him in water, such is their trust in the return of their souls to another body. Their custom is to cremate the dead.

Accounts of the Island of Sarandīb and of the Region of al-Aghbāb, Which Faces It

In the island of Sarandīb (where the mountain of gems, the pearl fishery, and so on are situated) certain Indian men[152] used to make so bold as to go into the market armed with the *jazbī*, a type of dagger of theirs, superbly crafted and finely honed; they would lunge at the most eminent merchant they could get hold of, grab him by the collar, pull the dagger on him, then march him out of town—and all in the middle of a crowd of people who could do nothing at all to stop him, because, if they tried to snatch the merchant from him, the abductor would kill both his captive and himself. Once away from town, the abductor would demand a ransom from the merchant, and someone would come after the latter and pay a large sum of money to secure his release. These kidnappings went on for a period of time, until a king ascended the throne who gave orders that any Indian committing this crime should be captured, whatever the cost. This was acted upon, and the Indian kidnapper would kill the merchant and then himself. The same happened to a considerable number of them, and the lives of both the Indian kidnappers and the Arab merchants were lost as a result. Then, when fear had befallen everyone, the abductions ceased, and the merchants felt safe again. 2.11.1 *The abduction of merchants*

The source from which their red, green, and yellow gemstones emerge is the Mountain of Sarandīb.[153] Sarandīb is an island, and the gems mostly appear to the people at times when the tide is high: water causes the stones to tumble down to them out of their caves, grottos, and watercourses, and these places are kept under surveillance by the king. Also, they sometimes mine the gems in the same way that minerals are mined; they come out embedded in rock, which has to be chipped away. 2.11.2 *Gemstones and how they obtain them*

The king of this island has a code of religious law and a corps of legal scholars specializing in it: they hold sessions like those of our scholars of hadith, in which the Indians[154] gather to take down 2.11.3 *Religions in Sarandīb* from the scholars' dictation the lives of their prophets and the laws contained in their legal codes. There is also a huge idol of pure gold, about whose weight sailors make stupendous claims, and temples on which huge sums of money are spent.[155] On this island, too, are large communities of Jews and followers of other religions, as well as Dualists. The king permits each of these denominations to live by its own laws.

2.11.4 *The Ghubb of Sarandīb, and the blessings of that land*

Facing this island are some wide *ghubb*s, *ghubb* meaning the course of a large river, provided it is extremely long and broad and has an outflow to the sea. People going along the particular *ghubb* known as the Ghubb of Sarandīb can travel for two months and more through woods and meadows where the climate is moderate. At the mouth of this *ghubb* lies the sea known as Harkand. It is a salubrious place; a sheep costs half a dirham there, and the drink prepared from palm "honey" with fresh hypericum seeds costs the same.[156]

2.11.5 *Gambling among the people of this land*

Their most frequent occupation is gambling at cock fights and backgammon. Their cocks have large bodies and well developed spurs; in addition, the people make use of sharpened miniature daggers, which they lash on to the birds' spurs before letting them loose. They gamble for gold, silver, land, slavegirls,[157] and other stakes, and a champion cock can be worth a huge amount of gold.

Similarly, their backgammon games are always played for very high stakes, to the extent that the indigent and penniless types among them, if they are the sort who go looking for ways to waste time and display their machismo, sometimes gamble their own fingertips away. This type of gambler, when he plays, keeps a container beside him into which walnut or sesame oil has been poured—olive oil is not to be found in their land—and beneath which a flame burns, heating the oil; between the two players lies a small, sharp ax. When one of them defeats his fellow player, the latter puts his hand on a stone, then the winner strikes one of the loser's fingertips with the ax and chops it off. The loser then dips his hand in the oil, which is now extremely hot, and cauterizes it. Nor does this stop him going back to the game; indeed, the players sometimes part having both lost all their fingertips.

Some players will also take the wick of a lamp, soak it thoroughly in the oil, place it on one of their limbs, then set fire to it. The wick smoulders away and the smell of burning flesh wafts about, while the player continues his backgammon game apparently undismayed.

2.11.6 *The sexual immorality of the people of this land*

Sexual immorality is rife in this place, among both women and men, and is not prohibited. It even happens that one of the seagoing merchants will sometimes invite a daughter of the king of these people to an assignation, and she will come to him in the forests, with the full knowledge of her father. The religious scholars in Sīrāf used to forbid their people from going on trading voyages to this region, and particularly the young men.

General Accounts of India Continued

2.12.1 *Monsoon rains and the cultivation of rice*

Concerning the *yasārah* that occurs in India, meaning the monsoon rain, it falls on their land continuously throughout the summer, for three consecutive months, night and day, the rainfall never letting up at all.[158] They lay in their basic provisions in advance of it, and, when the *yasārah* comes, they stay put in their houses, because they are solidly built of wood and have roofs which they keep swept with brooms[159] and which are thatched with certain types of native grass. No one ventures out, except for some pressing need; craftsmen, however, ply their trades in these places throughout the period of the rains. Sometimes the soles of their feet rot in this season.

Their livelihood depends on this *yasārah*; if it fails, they perish. This is because they grow rice alone: they know no other crop, and have no other staple food. The rice grows only at this time in their *ḥarām*s, thrown down haphazardly, with no need for them to irrigate it or take care of it (*ḥarām*s meaning "rice fields" in their language). When their skies become clear at the end of the monsoon rains, the rice is at its most abundant and plentiful. In winter, no rain falls on their land.

2.12.2 *Brahmans, conjurors, and others*

Among the Indians are religious devotees and men of learning known as brahmans, as well as poets who frequent the courts of kings, astrologers, philosophers, soothsayers, and those who take auguries from the flight of crows and other birds.[160] In India there are also conjurors and illusionists who are masters of their art; they are particularly to be found at Qannawj, a large city in the kingdom of al-Jurz.

2.12.3 *The bīkarjīs*

In India there is a group known as the *bīkarjīs*. They are naked, although their hair is so long that it covers their upper bodies and pudenda. They let their fingernails grow as long as spearheads, for they are never clipped, or only if they get broken, and they live a life of wandering. Each of them wears a cord around his neck from which a human skull is suspended. When one of them becomes unbearably hungry he stops at the door of one of the Indians, and they rush out to him bringing cooked rice, for they regard his coming as a blessing. He eats the rice out of the skull, and when he has had enough he goes away and will not ask for food again until he feels the need for it.

2.12.4 *Roadside prostitutes and "idol prostitutes"*

The Indians have various sorts of religious practices by which they propitiate, or so they claim, their Creator—glorious is God, and exalted far beyond what the evildoers say![161] One of these practices is for someone to build a roadside shop for travelers and to install in it a shopkeeper from whom passers-by can buy what they need and to install in the same shop an Indian woman as a prostitute. The builder of the shop pays her expenses, and passing travelers can enjoy her favors. This "benefaction" they consider an act for which they will be divinely rewarded.

In India there are also prostitutes known as "idol prostitutes."[162] The reason for this is that, if a woman who has made a vow gives birth to a pretty baby daughter, she takes it to the *budd*—that is, the idol that they worship—and dedicates her daughter to it.[163] In time, she finds her daughter a room in the market, hangs a curtain over the door, and sits the girl on a chair in front of the curtain. This is so that Indians and others of all sects may call on her—those, that is, who allow themselves such license in their religion—and the girl will make herself available for a standard fee. Whenever her takings reach a certain amount, she hands them over to the idol's sacristans to be spent on the fabric of the temple. And God, glorious and mighty is He, we praise for the guidance He chose for us and by which He purified us from the sins of the unbelievers!

2.12.5 *The idol of al-Multān*

Regarding the idol known as al-Multān, which is near al-Manṣūrah, devotees will travel for many months to visit it. A visitant will carry with him Indian aloewood of the Qāmarūnī variety (Qāmarūn is a region in which excellent aloewood is found) in order to bring it to this idol and present it to the sacristans for the censing of the idol. This aloewood can be worth two hundred dinars a maund,[164] and it is sometimes so saturated with resin that one can press a seal ring into the wood and it will retain the impression. Merchants buy it from these sacristans.[165]

2.12.6 *The blessings of the coconut palm*

In India there are certain pious people whose religious practices include that of traveling to the islands that are created in the sea, planting coconut palms on them and providing sources of freshwater, all with a view to divine reward. If ships put into these islands, they can enjoy the benefits of the palms. Indeed, in Oman there are shipwrights who travel to these islands where the coconut palms are, bringing with them carpentry tools and other equipment. They fell as much coconut wood as they want; when it is dry, it is sawn into planks. Next, using the coconut fiber, they twist enough cordage to sew together the planks they have sawn, and use them to build the hull of a ship.[166] They then hew masts from the coconut wood, weave sails from its fronds, and use its fiber to twist what they call *kharābāt*, which are cables in our parlance. When they have finished all this, the ships are loaded with coconuts and sailed to Oman, where the nuts are sold. The blessings and advantages of the coconut palm are great indeed, for all these products come from it and do not need to be supplemented from any other source.

The Land of the Zanj

2.13.1 *Crops, warriors, and the awe in which the Arabs are held*

The land of the Zanj is extensive. All the millet that grows there and is their staple food, as well as the sugar cane and other plants—all their varieties of these crops are black in color. They are ruled by kings who raid each other. These kings have warriors known as the Pierced Ones, whose noses are pierced and fitted with rings to which chains are attached. In time of war they advance; each chain, however, has a man holding on to the other end of it and tugging at it—this is to hold the warriors back from advancing until envoys have gone out to mediate between the two sides. If peace is made, there the matter ends; if not, the warriors are let loose with the chains bound around their necks, and battle is joined. Nothing can stand up to these fighters, and nothing less than death itself will cause one of them to desert his post.

The Zanj feel great awe in their hearts for the Arabs. If they catch sight of an Arab, they prostrate themselves before him and say, "This man is from a kingdom where the date tree grows!" This is because of the prestige that dates enjoy, both in their land and in their hearts.

2.13.2 *Zanj preachers*

The Zanj have a talent for sermons; indeed, no other nation has preachers like theirs, when they preach in their own tongues. There are those of them who devote themselves to a life of piety; wearing the skin of a leopard or a monkey and holding a staff, such a man will approach the people, and a crowd will gather around him. He will then stand there, remaining on his feet all day until nightfall, preaching to them, calling on them to keep God in their minds—may His honorable name be exalted—and describing to them the fate of their people who have died.

It is from their land that Zanjī leopards are exported.[167] They are notable for their reddish color and excellent breeding, as well as for their ample size.

The Island of Socotra

2.14.1 In the sea lies an island known as Socotra, where the Socotri aloes grow;[168] it is situated near both the land of the Zanj and the land of the Arabs. Most of its inhabitants are Christians. The reason for this is that, when Alexander conquered the empire of Persia, his tutor Aristotle would write to him to inform him of the various lands he had come across in his researches. In the course of this correspondence, Aristotle wrote to Alexander telling him that he should seek out an island in the sea known as Socotra, and that it was where aloes grow, aloes being the sovereign remedy without which no laxative is complete. The correct course of action, Aristotle advised, was to expel the inhabitants of the island and to resettle it with Greeks who could keep guard over it, so that the aloes could be exported from there to the Levant, Asia Minor,[169] and Egypt. Alexander therefore dispatched a force, expelled the islanders, and settled a body of Greeks on the island. He also gave orders to the factional rulers in Persia[170]—who, following the death of Darius the Great at his hands, were as yet obedient to his commands—to keep the settlers under their protection. The position of the settlers thus remained secure. In time, when God sent Jesus as a prophet, eternal peace be upon him, news of his mission reached the Greeks living on these islands[171] and they, along with the mass of the Romans, adopted Christianity. Their remaining descendants live on the island to this day, alongside other races who have settled there.[172]

Seas and Lands Lying West of the Gulf of Oman

2.15.1 In this book, meaning the First Book, the author did not mention the seas that lie to starboard of ships when they leave Oman and the land of the Arabs and sail out into the middle of the ocean. Only those seas lying to port were covered—that is, those comprising the Sea of India and China—for that was the intention of the person from whom that First Book was taken down.[173]

2.15.2 *The coasts between al-Shiḥr and al-Zaylaʿ*

On this sea that extends to starboard of India, from the view point of a ship leaving Oman,[174] lies the land of al-Shiḥr. In it are the places where frankincense grows, and it is one of the territories of ʿĀd, Ḥimyar, Jurhum, and the Tubbaʿs. The people there speak ancient ʿĀdite dialects of Arabic, and the Arabs do not understand most of their speech.[175] They have no settlements, even as small as villages, and live harsh and straitened lives. Their territory continues up to that of Aden and the coasts of Yemen; the coast then continues to Jidda, and from Jidda to al-Jār and the coast of al-Shaʾm. The coast then carries on to al-Qulzum, and there the sea comes to an end;[176] it is the place about which God, may His honorable name be exalted, said in the Qurʾan, «And He has placed between the two seas a barrier.»[177] The coast of the sea then turns back from al-Qulzum towards the land of the Barbar and connects with the western side of the Sea of al-Qulzum, which faces the land of Yemen. It continues past the land of Abyssinia—from where Barbarī leopard skins are exported, which are the best and most flawless skins available—then passes al-Zaylaʿ, where ambergris and *dhabl* (turtle shells) are to be found.

2.15.3 *The perils of the Sea of al-Qulzum, and the blessings of the Sea of India and China*

If the ships of the Sīrāfīs reach this sea that lies to starboard of the Sea of India and then go on to Jidda, they remain there; meanwhile, cargoes of theirs bound for Egypt are transferred to the ships of al-Qulzum. The reason is that the Sīrāfīs' vessels are not suited to sailing this sea of al-Qulzum, because of the difficulty of navigating it and the numerous rocks that protrude from its waters; in addition, there are no kings[178] and no inhabited places anywhere on its shores. Ships sailing this sea must look for a place to take shelter every night, for fear of the rocks in it, so they sail only by day and anchor at night. It is a dismal, hostile, and malodorous sea,[179] and there is no good to be found in its depths or on its surface, unlike the Sea of India and China, in whose depths are pearls and ambergris, in whose rocky isles are gems and mines of gold, in the mouths of whose beasts is ivory, in whose forests grow ebony, sapan wood, rattans, and trees that bear aloewood, camphor, nutmeg, cloves, sandalwood, and all manner of fragrant and aromatic spices, whose birds are *fafaghā* (parrots, that is) and peacocks, and the creeping things of whose earth are civet cats and musk gazelles, and all the rest that no one could enumerate, so many are its blessings.

Ambergris and Whales

On the subject of ambergris, such as that which is cast up on the shores of this sea on the western side of the Sea of India, it is a substance that is driven there by the waves but originates further out in the Sea of India, although it is not known where it emerges from.[180] The finest quality is the sort that is cast up at Barbarā and on the shores bordering the land of the Zanj, as well as at al-Shiḥr and the adjoining coast: it is found in the form of "eggs,"[181] rounded and bluish-gray. The people of these regions have thoroughbred camels, and on moonlit nights they mount them and ride out along their shores; the camels are specially trained and taught how to scan the shore for ambergris, and, when they spot some, they kneel so that their riders can dismount and pick it up. Ambergris is also found floating on the surface of the sea in lumps of great weight, sometimes up to the size of a bull. If the whale known as the *bāl* sees this floating ambergris, it swallows it;[182] when it reaches its stomach it causes the death of the whale, which then floats on the surface of the water. There are people who keep a lookout for this from boats and who know the times when these ambergris-swallowing whales are to be found. When they catch sight of one, they haul it ashore with iron grapnels attached to stout ropes, which stick into the whale's back, in order to cut it open and extract the ambergris from it. Any of the ambergris that has been in contact with the whale's stomach is *mand*, the sort with the rancid and fishy smell[183] stocked by the druggists in Madinat al-Salām and Basra; any ambergris uncontaminated by the rancidness of the whale's stomach will be extremely pure. 2.16.1

Sometimes the vertebrae of this whale known as the *bāl* are used to make seats: a person can sit on one of these and fit snugly into it. Informants have reported, too, that at a village ten *farsakh*s distant from Sīrāf, known as al-Tāyin, there are some ancient small houses roofed with the bones of this whale.[184] I also heard someone say that, in days of old, one of these whales was washed up near Sīrāf; he went to have a look at it and found people climbing on to its back with a small ladder. If fishermen get hold of one, they leave it in the sun, cut up its flesh, and dig trenches for this flesh so that the whale oil will accumulate in them. The oil is also scooped out of the whale's eye with jars, once the eye has been melted by the sun.[185] All this oil is collected and sold to the owners of ships; it is then mixed with various other ingredients that they use and daubed on the hulls of the seagoing ships to seal the seams in the planking and to seal any places where the seams have come apart.[186] The oil of this whale fetches a considerable sum of money.

An Account of Pearls

2.17.1 *The formation of pearls* The genesis of pearls comes about under the beneficent direction of God, may His name be blessed. For it is He that says in the Qur'an, mighty and exalted is He, «Glory be to Him who has created all the pairs of that which the earth sends forth, and of humankind themselves, and of that which they do not know.»[187] When pearl oysters first come into being, they are similar in size to an asafoetida leaf and of similar color, shape, smallness, lightness, delicacy, and fragility.[188] While in this state, they flit over the surface of the water until they alight on the sides of the pearl divers' boats. With the passing days, they grow stronger and bigger, and gradually turn hard like stone. When they are heavy enough, they sink and attach themselves to the seabed; God knows best what they get their sustenance from. The oysters contain nothing but a piece of pinkish flesh, like a tongue, attached to the base of their shells, with neither bone nor sinew and having no vein in it. Opinions have differed as to how the pearl first comes into being. Some have said that when rain falls, the oysters appear on the surface of the water and open their mouths; this is so that drops of rain will fall into them and become pearls. Others have said, however, that the pearls are generated from the oyster itself. This is the more accurate of the two accounts, because pearls are often found in the oyster when they are still sprouting up and have not yet become separated from the nacreous lining of the shell. They are pried off by the pearlers and are what the seagoing merchants term "pried pearls."[189] And God knows best which of the two accounts is correct.

2.17.2 *The tale of the oyster and the fox*

Among the various amazing accounts we have heard of how God sustains His creatures in unexpected ways[190] is that of a bedouin who, in days of old, arrived in Basra with a pearl that was worth a large amount of money. He took it to a druggist of his acquaintance, showed it to him, and asked him what it was; he himself had no idea of its value. The druggist told him that the object was a pearl. "What is it worth?" the bedouin asked. "A hundred dirhams," the druggist replied. The bedouin thought this an enormous sum. "Would anyone actually give me that much for it?" he asked. The druggist immediately paid him a hundred dirhams, and the bedouin went off and bought provisions for his family. The druggist, meanwhile, took the pearl to Madīnat al-Salām and sold it there for a large amount of money, with which he was able to expand his business.

The druggist mentioned that he asked the bedouin how he had come by the pearl. "I was passing al-Ṣammān," the bedouin told him—this being part of the land of Bahrain,[191] a short distance from the seashore—"when I saw a fox lying dead on the sand. I noticed that something had attached itself to the fox's muzzle, so I went down to it and found the thing was like a dish with a lid, all gleaming white inside. Then I found this round thing in it, and I took it." On hearing this, the druggist realized what had happened. The oyster had left the sea and gone on to the shore to sniff the wind, as oysters are accustomed to do. The fox had passed by and spotted the piece of flesh inside the oyster's open mouth, and had then pounced with all swiftness, stuck its muzzle in the oyster and sunk its teeth into the flesh inside. At this the oyster had snapped shut on the fox's muzzle. (It is in the nature of oysters, if they have thus clamped shut on something and then sense a hand touching them, that nothing will induce them to open their mouths—until, that is, they are split apart with an iron blade: this is the oyster's way of holding on to its pearl and protecting it, as a mother protects her baby.) When the oyster had begun to suffocate the fox, the fox had rushed about, hitting the oyster on the ground, right and left. Eventually the oyster had succeeded in suffocating the fox; the fox had died, and the oyster had died too. Then the bedouin had got hold of the oyster and taken the pearl that was in it, and God had led him to the druggist. And thus the oyster proved to be the bedouin's windfall.

Further Accounts of Indian Customs

2.18.1 *Their habit of adorning themselves with gems and of carrying parasols*

The kings of India wear in their ears pendants of precious gems set in gold and adorn their necks with precious necklaces comprising magnificent red and green gems and pearls, all of which are enormously costly and valuable and which today represent their treasure and their reserves of wealth; the commanders of their armies and other prominent men also wear such jewelry. The most important Indian dignitaries ride about on men's backs, wearing nothing but a waist cloth to make themselves decent, and holding a thing known as a *chatrah*,[192] which is a parasol of peacock feathers that they carry to protect themselves from the sun. Thus they ride, surrounded by their entourage.

2.18.2 *Some customs concerning food*

There is a class of Indians of whom two will not eat together out of the same dish or even at the same table; they would consider it a most dreadful disgrace to do so. If they came to Sīrāf and one of the prominent merchants invited them to a meal—even as many as a hundred of them, or less, or more—the host would have to place a dish in front of each man, with his own food in it, so that no one else would have to share it with him.[193] In the case of kings and other important people in their own country, new tables are provided for them every day, and the fronds of coconut palms are woven together and made into the equivalent of crockery and serving dishes. When the main meal is served, they eat their food off these woven palm fronds, and, when they have finished their meal, both the table and the woven palm-frond "crockery" are thrown, together with any remaining food, into water. The following day they start all over again with fresh utensils.

In the past, Sindī dinars used to be exported to the Indians; the exchange rate for one of them was three standard dinars and more. Emeralds originating in Egypt are exported to them, set in signet rings and encased in small boxes. *Bussadh* (coral) is also exported there. A stone called *dahnaj* used to be exported there, too; then they abandoned it. **2.18.3** *Dinars and gemstones exported to India*

Most of the kings of India, when they hold audiences, have their womenfolk with them on public display, to be seen by all comers whether native or foreign. They are not concealed from view. **2.18.4** *The display in public of royal ladies*

Afterword to the Second Book

This Second Book, then, is the best part of what my memory has been able to recollect at the time, given the wide range of accounts of the sea.[194] I have avoided relating any of the sort of accounts in which sailors exercise their powers of invention but whose credibility would not stand up to scrutiny in other men's minds. I have also restricted myself to relating only the true contents of each account—and the shorter the better.[195] And God it is who guides us to what is correct. **2.19.1** *Abū Zayd's afterword*

And praise be to God, Lord of the universe, and may His blessings be upon the choicest part of His creation, Muḥammad, and on all his family. God is our sufficiency and our best support and aid.[196]

Notes

1 The English-language synopses and chapter headings have been supplied by the editor-translator and are not part of the original Arabic text.

2 The opening pages of the book are lost, including the section on the First Sea (i.e., the Arabian/Persian Gulf; cf. al-Masʿūdī, *Murūj*, 1:149) and the beginning of that on the Second Sea. Here the author is describing a whale.

3 *Minārah*, "lighthouse," is also used for (and is the origin of the English word) "minaret." Whales spray water from their blowholes, not from their mouths.

4 Some whales do indeed smack the water with their tails, to stun and concentrate their prey before swallowing them, a behavior known as "kick feeding." Recent studies have regarded it as a learned behavior unique to North Atlantic humpback whales (http://www.internationalwhaleprotection.org/forum/index.php?/topic/3057-chapter-86-the-tail/).

5 *Nawāqīs*, wooden clappers, were used in Eastern churches as "bells" (Ibn Baṭṭūṭah, *Travels*, 2:470 n. 214).

6 The length of a cubit was subject to local variation. Taking it as 47.5 centimeters (a general standard for a builder's cubit, cf. Serjeant and Lewcock, *Ṣanʿāʾ*, 468), this would make the *wāl* 9.5 meters long.

7 The real origin of ambergris, a valuable fixative for perfumes, is even stranger: it is a waxy substance exuded by the intestines of sperm whales, usually as a result of irritation caused by the undigested beaks of cuttlefish or giant squid (Cheung and DeVantier, *Natural History*, 212).

8 That is, they are animals, not plants.

9 The most celebrated pearl fisheries were in the Gulf of Mannar, in northwestern Sri Lanka (Tennent, *Ceylon*, 2:560).

10 Unless the reading is defective, this seems to mean that open sea surrounds it so that it has no near neighbors, unlike the Maldives and Laccadives.

11 Seventy cubits (ca. 33 m.) is a huge exaggeration. Ibn Baṭṭūṭah (*Travels*, 4:854) gives eleven spans (ca. 2.25 m.). Skeen (*Adam's Peak*, 203) found the alleged footprint to be five feet seven inches (ca. 1.70 m.) long.

12 The reference to two kings alludes to the age-old division of influence between Sinhala and Tamil rule in Sri Lanka.

13 Aloewood is the fragrant and highly prized resinous heartwood of trees of the genus *Aquilaria*.

14 Arabic *shank* is the same word as English "chank" (*Turbinella rapa*). Chank fishing remained a government monopoly into the nineteenth century (Tennent, *Ceylon*, 2:556).

15 The use of *maʿādin*, usually meaning "mines, sources of minerals," for camphor as well as gold may suggest that the writer believed camphor to be of mineral origin. The substance, although crystalline, comes from the camphor tree.

16 *Caesalpina sappan* produces a valuable red dye (Yule and Burnell, *Hobson-Jobson*, s.v. "Sappan-Wood"). Rattans are various types of pliable cane.

17 An interpolation may have occurred (*ilayhi min* instead of simply *ilā*). Without it, the sense would agree with the rest of the paragraph: "And they do not need coverings for their bodies, because it is neither hot nor cold." Alternatively, a phrase may have been omitted, and the original may have read along these lines: "and such coverings as they need for their bodies, *and these are few*, as it is neither hot nor cold in their land."

18 Literally, "peppercorn-like."

19 The parenthetical comment is strange, although it may be that *qadam* (foot) is used here as a slang term for the penis.

20 The accusation of cannibalism persisted into the time of Marco Polo (*Travels*, 2:309) and beyond.

21 The most powerful types of waterspout, such as that described here, are tornadoes occurring over the sea. Although they do not in fact draw up water, they can pose a danger to smaller craft.

22 That is, from the northwest, the Big Dipper (Arabic *banāt al-naʿsh*) being the seven brightest stars in Ursa Major, the prominent constellation in the northern sky.

23 A reference to phosphorescence, a common phenomenon in Indian Ocean waters.

24 Apparent lacuna in text, perhaps caused by a missing leaf or leaves.

25 Text defective.

26 Given the distance from the Arabian/Persian Gulf to China and the risk of missing the right sailing season (*mawsim*, the origin of "monsoon") for a particular stage of the voyage, it was possible to be held up by adverse winds for many months.

27 Prayers for the Muslim ruler, pronounced during the sermon at Friday congregational worship and at the two ʿĪds, or festivals, were a sign of political allegiance to him.

28 As Hourani points out (*Arab Seafaring*, 75), "China ships," that is, large vessels from the Gulf specializing in the China trade, is more accurate than "Chinese ships," ships from China. Cf. the term "Indiamen" for European ships involved in the East India trade.

29 That is, the Arabian/Persian Gulf.

30 The verb *khaṭifa* most commonly means "to take quickly and unexpectedly, to snatch." Although "to set sail" is among its classical senses (Lane, *Lexicon*, s.v. *khaṭifa*) it is a rare one, which "take off" attempts to reflect.

31 Jibāl ʿUmān is literally "the mountains of Oman." At sea, however, a *jabal* can be anything from a flat coral island to a towering rock stack. Here, part of the fjord-like coast of the Musandam Peninsula and its outlying islets may be intended.

32 This *durdūr* (whirpool) is described in greater detail by al-Idrīsī (*Nuzhah*, 1:164). It is not specifically mentioned in the later

navigational texts, although Aḥmad ibn Mājid warns of "strong currents" in these waters (Tibbetts, *Arab Navigation*, 213).

33 From here on, the sailing times appear to include the time needed to put into port, do business, load supplies, etc. For comparison, *Sohar*, a sailing ship constructed on the lines of early Arab vessels, took twenty-eight days from Muscat to Calicut (not far north of Kollam), including a stop of some days for repairs in the Laccadives (Severin, *Sindbad Voyage*, 6).

34 The alcoholic version of the drink is the Anglo-Indian "toddy."

35 "Payment . . . on the spot" is the classical sense of *yadan bi-yad*, literally "hand in hand" (Lane, *Lexicon*, s.v. *yad*).

36 Arabic *fūṭah*, the Malay *sarong*.

37 The Zhu Jiang, or Pearl River.

38 In contrast to the earlier reference (1.1.1) in which flying fish are given a Persian name for "locust," here the usual Arabic word, *jarād*, is used.

39 This palm-climbing "fish"—the Arabic word being used here to mean "sea creature"—must be the aptly named coconut crab.

40 Does this reflect a difference in caste from the other Indian princes? *Sharaf*, the "high rank, nobility" that Dahmā lacks and in which his fellow-king Balharā excels, is often a matter of ancestry.

41 The Arabic which this last phrase tentatively translates is obscure. A small emendation, however, could make the sentence read: "By nature this rhinoceros [ranges from being] smaller than the elephant up to the same [size] as it." This statement would be no stranger than the claim, below, that the animal has no joints in its legs. In Ibn Baṭṭūṭah's equally strange perception (*Travels*, 3:596) the rhinoceros is "smaller than an elephant, but its head is many times bigger than an elephant's head."

42 Such belts, in vogue under the Tang dynasty, were of leather decorated with rhinoceros-horn plaques (Sauvaget, *Relation*, 54).

43 The word *fakhūr*, "proud," is voweled as such in the manuscript but may be a scribal error for *fa-khawr*, "and then [comes] a bay/estuary," that is, where the ambergris of the next phrase is found.

44 This suggests that there is not enough pepper to be dried for storage and/or export and that it is eaten fresh as a local delicacy.

45 In China, eunuch officials were in charge of taxes and financial affairs in general (see below, 2.3.5).

46 That is, al-Mābud is the last of the kingdoms before one reaches Chinese territory.

47 "King" in the sense of "[provincial] ruler"; hereafter "ruler" is used to translate it. On eunuch officials, see above, n. 45.

48 *Ṣīniyyāt* (chinaware) most frequently refers, as in English, to ceramics. Here, however, Chinese lacquerware is probably intended (cf. Sauvaget, *Relation*, 56 n.33.3). The instrument's length of 3–4 cubits equals about 142.5–190 cm.

49 Literally, "They have indicators and regulation for the hours." Public water clocks were known in Tang Dynasty China.

50 "Copper coins," Arabic *fulūs* (sg. *fils*), are small copper-alloy coins of low value, pierced in the middle for stringing on a cord, and later known in English as "cash."

51 This succinct description is, apparently, the first known one of porcelain in a text from the West (Sauvaget, *Relation*, 57 n. 34.5).

52 The indemnity granted to the sea merchants (literally "sea men", i.e., traders from overseas) presumably guarantees compensation for any harm befalling their goods while in the government warehouses. The point of the six-month delay is that, at the end of that period, contrary winds mean no more merchants will come until the following sailing season; releasing all the goods into the market simultaneously means that their prices can be controlled.

53 The Anglo-Indian "maund," Arabic *mann(ā)*, is a unit of weight that varies greatly. That here intended is probably a little more than two pounds (1 kg.) (Yule and Burnell, *Hobson-Jobson*, s.v. "Maund").

54 Not, here, the fragrant wood (see n. 13 above), but the juice of succulent plants of the genus *Aloe*.

55 The implication being, "Well, you'll grieve for them *now*!" Three years was the official period of mourning for a deceased parent (Whitfield, *Silk Road*, 146).

56 Some phrases in the following paragraph are open to different interpretation. It is not always entirely clear which of the two parties the various pronouns and verbs refer to; the problem is exacerbated by the text's customarily compressed wording, as well as by some loose syntax.

57 The sense of a mark made *bayna*, "between," two fingers is not clear. The historian Rashīd al-Dīn (d. 718/1318) mentions outlines of fingers traced as identifying marks in China; there is also evidence of the use, as early as the Tang Dynasty, of fingerprints as marks (Yule, *Cathay,* 3:123–24). If the latter is intended here, then various emendations might be proposed for *bayna*, e.g., *tubayyinu/tubīnu*, "showing clearly," or even *banāni*, "of the fingertips of."

58 Going by the (correct) information given below (2.3.3), namely that one *fakkūj* equals about one dinar, the figure here should be amended to twenty thousand dinars.

59 Reading *yajzuzna*, "cut, crop" (although other readings are possible). The implication is not that they have their hair cut *off*, but rather that it is cut and styled, unlike, say, Arab women, who allow their hair to grow freely. Cf. the illustration of Tang women's hairstyles in Whitfield, *Silk Road*, 145.

60 The foregoing passage on royal funeral rites appears, with a few additions, in *Murūj al-dhahab* (al-Masʿūdī, 1:83–84), introduced by the words, "I have seen in the land of Sarandīb . . . that when a king of theirs dies . . ." Given that al-Masʿūdī clearly borrowed the account, the phrasing is more than a little arch, with its suggestion, if not categorical statement, that he witnessed the scene himself.

61 That is, the last of the Dībājāt (today's Laccadives, Maldives, and Sri Lanka) when approached from the Arabian/Persian Gulf. Cf. 1.2.2, above.

62 "Tiger or leopard" is Arabic *numūr*, which can refer to either or both.

63 *Tasil . . . min*, "melted from," might possibly be amended to *tusmal . . . min*, "been put out by."

64 The appointment of crown princes would facilitate succession in the ruling dynasty.

65 As indicated above (1.7.2), he is "king of kings" not in the imperial sense, but rather in that of "king senior in precedence."

66 That is, the Malabar Coast of southwestern India, corresponding approximately with the modern state of Kerala. John Keay (*A History of India*, p. 191) suggests that the the forcible annexation referred to may be a memory of the seizure of the Chalukyan kingdom of Karnataka by Krishna I, the second/eighth-century ruler of the Rashtrakuta state.

67 "As his puppet": the Arabic phrase is, literally, "from under his hand."

68 There is evidence that certain body parts of executed criminals were indeed eaten and that the practice continued down at least to the nineteenth century (Sauvaget, *Relation*, 64 n. 56.2).

69 A slightly different style of impalement was described by Ibn Baṭṭūṭah (*Travels*, 4:806) as the penalty, in southwestern India, for stealing a single coconut.

70 *Zawānī l-bidadah*, literally "the harlots of the idols," are the women known in India as *devadasis*. See also 2.12.4 below.

71 "Neither . . . nor . . . are users of carpets," Arabic *laysa . . . bi-ʾaṣḥābi furshin*. Sauvaget (*Relation*, 65 n. 61.1) and his predecessors have taken *fursh* to mean "wives, concubines," a euphemistic usage: *fursh* are "mats, carpets, mattresses, furnishings, beds," and thus, by extension, "bed*fellows*." It seems preferable, however, to take the phrase as belonging to the section on buildings and to translate it as some sort of literal furnishing. "Carpets" may well be the intention, as their absence would be of particular interest to an Arabic reader for whom carpets were ubiquitous.

72 A good example of how the informants' purview did not extend to the inland, wheat-eating areas of northern India.

73 "The two provinces"—*al-wilāyatayn* (an unusual word to refer to the two countries)—suggests that the previous sentence should end "China *and India*." "Leopards, tigers" at the beginning of that sentence again gets around the multiple meanings of *numūr* (see n. 62, above).

74 In the Islamic legal context, probably intended here too, "those who 'cut the road'" include rebels and other malefactors as well as highway robbers.

75 *Janābah* is a state of bodily pollution, most commonly caused by sexual activity. For a Muslim, it necessitates washing the entire body before one is permitted to pray.

76 "More densely inhabited and cultivated": *aʿmar* means either or both; one might also add "and built up."

77 In the Chinese context, therapeutic burning, Arabic *kayy*, is probably the practice known as moxibustion. Another form, still occasionally practiced in the Arab world, involves burning the patient with small branding irons on certain parts of the body.

78 *ʿIlm al-nujūm*, "the science of the stars," is another of those single terms that has more than one meaning in present-day English—hence "astronomy and astrology."

79 If by this singular "king of India" Balharā is meant, the information here would contradict the earlier statement (above, 1.7.2) that he pays his troops.

80 "Our rivers," given the context, probably includes the Tigris and the Euphrates.

81 This may be a reference to the long belted tunic in vogue under the Tang Dynasty and called the *hufu*, or "foreigner's robe." Cf. the illustrations in Whitfield, *Silk Road*, 89 and 107.

82 Here, in the margin of the manuscript, is a note added, in a poor hand, some four hundred years after the book was copied: "This book was checked by al-Faqīr Muḥammad in the year 1011 [1602–3], may God bless with goodness the year that follows and those that come after. Amen. And may God forgive the writer of these lines his sins, and those of his parents too, and of all the Muslims."

83 "Its kings" is shorthand for "the kings of its islands and of the lands on and beyond its shores."

84 Al-Masʿūdī (1:138) puts the number of foreigners killed in Khānfū at 200,000.

85 Huang Chao took the imperial capital, Chang'an, in the fall of 267/880 (Whitfield, *Silk Road*, 150).

86 Huang Chao did in fact proclaim himself emperor.

87 “They are . . . kinsmen by marriage”: it is not wholly clear whether the relationship is between the Chinese and the Taghazghuz, or between the Taghazghuz and the rest of the Turks. If the former is meant, however, the phrase probably refers to marriages contracted earlier in the third/ninth century between women of the Tang imperial family and chiefs of the Turkic Uighurs, the Taghazghuz of the text (cf. Whitfield, *Silk Road*, 95 and 98).

88 The son of “the king of the Taghazghuz” was, in fact, the son of a chieftain of a powerful Turkic tribe, the Shatuo/Shato. This commander is known to the Chinese histories as Li Keyong. Al-Masʿūdī (*Murūj*, 1:139) gives the number of troops under his command as 400,000. Huang Chao is usually said to have cut his own throat before he could be captured, in the summer of 271/884 (Whitfield, *Silk Road*, 152).

89 “Pronounced the customary formulae of allegiance”: literally, “prayed for him [sc. at Friday prayers],” in an Islamic context, the usual way of publicly declaring official fealty to the caliph.

90 “Factional rulers” is either a reference to the satraps through whom Alexander ruled Persia or to his generals who were to squabble over his empire as a whole after his death. (Below, 2.14.1, the phrase clearly refers to the satraps.)

91 Cf. n. 68, above.

92 “The sea itself became uncooperative”: the phrase is taken from a saying, attributed to ʿAlī ibn Abī Ṭālib, predicting economic disaster.

93 A slightly ironical sense of *zuhdahā*, “her renunciation,” which normally refers to the renunciation of earthly pleasure for a life of pious asceticism.

94 *Ḥilyatahā*, translated here as “her physical appearance,” more often means “her ornaments, her jewelry,” etc., and might do so here. Alternatively, it could be a slip for *ḥillatahā*, “her [city] quarter.”

95 Revenues could be considerable: high-class courtesans, known as “mistresses of the table,” would charge sixteen thousand copper cash per evening (Whitfield, *Silk Road*, 147).

96 "All manner of attire": Arabic *alwān* means both "types, sorts, manners" and "colors." The latter may be implied here too.

97 The weight of one thousand copper cash was more than than 1.5 pounds (0.68 kg.) (Whitfield, *Silk Road*, 173).

98 Chinese coins have indeed turned up in the excavations at Sīrāf (Whitehouse, "Siraf," 143).

99 *Shiqāq*, "panels," are usually the pieces of heavy hair cloth that go together to make a tent. Here, however, they are clearly the panels of woven reed used in the reed architecture of southern Iraq, where the author lived.

100 On wooden clappers, see n. 5 above.

101 As it stands, the Arabic is slightly defective in the latter part of this sentence. The translation depends on a minor amendment.

102 Presumably, Abū Zayd included the second part of this sentence for the benefit of his Muslim readers who were not generally accustomed to seeing images of living creatures or only to seeing stylized depictions of them.

103 Basra was destroyed in 257/871, during the so-called Zanj Rebellion.

104 Presumably, the king refers to himself in the third person here because he is telling the interpreter what to say; immediately below, he returns to the first person. (In any case, this whole section containing Ibn Wahb's report is especially inconsistent in its use of grammatical persons and pronouns.)

105 Al-Masʿūdī explains in a parallel passage (*Murūj*, 1:143) that this is because the Turks are "the beasts of mankind."

106 To a Muslim readership the question would not seem strange: the Islamic aversion to depicting living beings applies in particular to the prophets, and, in the case of the Prophet Muḥammad, amounts to an outright ban.

107 It is customary for Muslims to utter a short prayer of blessing whenever a prophet is mentioned.

108 As a Muslim, Ibn Wahb would have believed that the Qur'anic/biblical Flood covered the whole earth.

109 "Thirty months" is a reflection of the relatively short public ministry of Jesus, beginning with his baptism.

110 The poses described are reminiscent of those of some of the figures of the Buddha and the Bodhisattvas, as depicted in Tang Dynasty images.

111 *Ziyy* is yet another word with more than one distinct sense in English, "outward appearance" and/or "clothing."

112 As it stands in the manuscript, the meaning of the second part of the sentence is a little obscure. With a small emendation to the Arabic it could mean, ". . . and his vizier too, and he scoffed and made it quite clear that he disapproved of what I had said."

113 "I blurted out": literally, "I [i.e., my tongue] slipped, and I said."

114 "Both in abode and in blood": literally, "in dwelling and in kinship."

115 In the later third/ninth century, Chang'an covered an area of about thirty square miles (ca. 78 sq. km.) and had a population of nearly two million (Whitfield, *Silk Road*, 146).

116 The Mediterranean is called here "the Sea of al-Shām" (i.e., of the Levant), in the next sentence "the Sea of al-Rūm" (of the Romans/Byzantines), and, a little further on, by both names together. The English name is used to avoid confusion. The Sea of China and India is the Indian Ocean; the ocean into which it leads is the Pacific.

117 The ships of the Arabs and other seafaring peoples of the western Indian Ocean were constructed without nails: the planks of the hulls were drilled, the corresponding holes of adjacent planks were "sewn" tightly together with coir rope, and all the seams and holes were thoroughly caulked. Severin (*Sindbad Voyage*, ch. 3) describes this ancient shipbuilding technique in detail. See also 2.12.6, below.

118 Abū Zayd has arrived at the right conclusion—that the Mediterranean Sea and Indian Ocean are connected—but by a very wrong route. Al-Masʿūdī, who drew on this passage, was well aware that the Caspian Sea does not connect with any other sea (*Murūj*, 1:125); he, too, suggests that the sewn planks must have floated around the north of the Eurasian landmass but implies that they entered the Mediterranean through the Strait of Gibraltar (*Murūj*, 1:163).

119 In this foregoing sentence, it seems that the word "except" is a slip and should be omitted, given the existence of the "barrier" (now penetrated by the Suez Canal) between the Red and Mediterranean Seas.

120 "The city of al-Zābaj," here and in the section title above, seems to be a slip for "The island of al-Zābaj."

121 "Extent" is used, here and below, to translate *taksīr*, properly speaking, "area." Nine hundred square *farsakh*s, however, is only a fraction of the actual area of Java, but it would be a far more accurate figure for the sailing distance *around* Java and the associated chain of islands to the east, and this may be what is intended.

122 *Al-raṣāṣ al-qalʿī* is commonly glossed as white lead, or cerussite, the main use of which was as a pigment. Yule and Burnell, however, argue (*Hobson-Jobson*, s.v. "Calay") that tin is meant.

123 That is, since the disturbances in China, Kalah [Bār] is the easternmost point to which Arab ships sail.

124 That is, there is no need to travel long stages, as in most of the lands of the Near East, because accommodation, food, etc., are available everywhere.

125 "They are men": reading *rijāl*. Other readings are possible, including *raḥḥālah*, "[frequent] travelers," and *rajjālah*, "travelers/fighters on foot."

126 What historical basis the following story may have (if any) is unclear. It could, however, be a mythicized memory of incursions into Cambodia at the end of the eighth century AD by the Sailendra dynasty of Java.

127 It is hard to explain the presence of this sentence. It may be corrupt, or a copyist may have inadvertently omitted words that would have given it context.

128 Properly speaking, "the throne," *al-sarīr*, is a low dais or divan such as the *gaddi* of Indian rulers.

129 This last phrase is obscure. With a small emendation to the voweling, the Arabic might mean, "so that those whom good health has clothed should make the most of it."

130 The Pool of the Kings, in the story above (2.6.2). On al-Mihrāj's throne, see n. 128, above.

131 That is, his face was now disfigured by smallpox scars.

132 See 1.8.8 above. In a parallel passage in al-Masʿūdī (*Murūj*, 1:141), the aggrieved Khurasani does not resort to ringing the bell but rather to wearing a garment of a particular type of red silk.

133 Trustworthy and thus, as becomes clear below, worthy of appointment as provincial judges.

134 This is a neat summary of Confucian concepts of government.

135 The desert is the Taklamakan.

136 The musk "gazelles" (in English musk "deer") are in fact neither true deer nor gazelles but belong to their own family, the *Moschidae*.

137 A Himalayan plant of the valerian family, from whose rhizome a costly perfume was made.

138 Musk is a secretion deposited in glands, the musk "pods," situated between the male animal's navel and its genitalia.

139 Clearly, Tibetan musk was imported into the Arab world overland and was thought to be a variety different from Chinese musk, which came by sea.

140 The musk deer does, in fact, rub its musk glands against trees and stones, to mark its territory and/or to attract mates. Whether this would deposit a harvestable amount of musk is to be doubted.

141 In fact, musk deer have neither horns nor antlers.

142 The "tusks" are, in fact, in the upper jaw and are elongated canines up to about seven centimeters long that point downward. *Fitr*, the Arabic unit of length translated as "the distance . . . stretched apart," is sometimes expressed in English as a "small span."

143 "Clipped": perhaps "docked."

144 All Abū Zayd's readers, male as well as female, would have squatted to urinate.

145 The phrase "allows its contents to well up," Arabic *tatfū bi-mā fīhā*, might be used of a scum rising to the surface in a cooking pot. The implication is that the noxious contents of the bladder can only be expelled in this way.

146 “Rounding” babies’ heads, that is, molding them into an evenly spherical shape while they are still malleable, is still practiced by the Arabs and other peoples and can be achieved by gentle binding and/or ensuring that the baby does not always sleep in the same position. Most if not all of Abū Zayd’s male readers would have kept their heads shaved or worn their hair short.

147 An allusion to Q Ḥujurāt 49:13, which states that God has made mankind into “peoples and tribes, that you may recognize one another.” (Is there an implied hint, in “among themselves,” of “. . . even if all the Chinese look the same to us non-Chinese”? The prejudice is an old one.) In contrast to the Chinese practice described in this section, Arabs will marry as close a relative as a first cousin.

148 Sandarac is the resin of a coniferous tree of the cypress family.

149 Literally, “at the head of his heart/internal organs.”

150 The storage jar called in Arabic *dann* is a type of large amphora.

151 The text does not say so, but we must assume he did it.

152 “Indian men”: clearly, here and below, local inhabitants of Sarandīb are meant. From the end of this section, it seems that the merchants involved were Arabs.

153 “The Mountain of Sarandīb” could stand for the highlands of Sri Lanka as a whole but means, in general, Adam’s Peak (see text, 1.2.2). The passage that follows implies a belief that tidal fluctuations had an affect on the level of subterranean water inland.

154 See n. 152, above, first sentence.

155 The idol of gold is a recurring theme in descriptions of Sarandīb (cf. Ibn Baṭṭūṭah on Dondra, *Travels*, 4:855–56, which may refer to the statue mentioned in this passage). Abū Zayd’s reluctance to give a weight for it reflects his policy to avoid “sailors’ yarns” (see text, 2.19.1).

156 *Hypericum* is a genus of shrubs also known as St. John’s wort. Regarding the first ingredient of the drink, other editions read *ʿasalu l-naḥl*, “bee honey,” for the *ʿasalu l-nakhl*, “palm ‘honey,’” of the manuscript. The dot of the *kh* is, admittedly, tentatively written in the manuscript, but it is far more likely to be correct, given the tradition of

palm tapping in the region (cf. Yule and Burnell, *Hobson-Jobson*, s.v. "Jaggery").

157 Other editions read *al-nabāt*, "plants, vegetation," where this editor reads *al-banāt*, "girls." The dots in the manuscript are too equivocally placed for a categorical decision, but the latter seem a more enticing prize.

158 "Rainfall" here is *shitāʾ*, meaning also "winter." At the end of this section, however, *shitāʾ* is used to signify the season.

159 "Roofs which they keep swept with brooms" is the immediately apparent meaning and hardly appropriate, given that the roofs are thatched. By reading *mukannanah* for *mukannasah*, however, the meaning would be "roofs with overhanging eaves," which would make more sense.

160 Taking auguries from the flight of birds, a practice called *zajr*, was a feature of ancient Arab life, which still has its Indian counterparts.

161 Cf. Q Isrāʾ 17:43.

162 See n. 70, above.

163 The sense of the "vow" is that the woman has made a request to the deity and has promised to dedicate to it any daughter she may give birth to, if her request is fulfilled.

164 See n. 53, above.

165 The implication being that the sacristans are corrupt.

166 See n. 117, above, on sewn ships.

167 Unless the text is defective, the animals themselves are intended here, not their skins.

168 See on aloes n. 54, above. Socotri aloes were supposedly the most efficacious as a medicine.

169 Asia Minor: Arabic al-Rūm, literally "[the land of] the Romans," but probably used here in the sense current in Abū Zayd's time, "[the land of] the Byzantines."

170 See on these factional rulers n. 90, above.

171 "These islands": the plural may be a slip, but there are, in fact, several lesser islands associated with Socotra, two of which currently have small populations.

172 Writing in the sixth century AD, the Alexandrian traveler Cosmas Indicopleustes (quoted in Cheung and DeVantier, *Natural History*, 228) noted the presence of Greek-speaking Christians on Socotra, whose ancestors, he says, were sent by Alexander's successors in Egypt, the Ptolemies.

173 This statement of Abū Zayd's may be taken to imply that he himself did not know the identity of the compiler of the First Book. See above, 5–7.

174 "To starboard of India, from the viewpoint of a ship leaving Oman" is a sailor's periphrasis for "To the west of India."

175 Six non-Arabic languages, classed as the Modern South Arabian group, are still found in the region. Each of the three major ones, Mehri, Soqotri, and Shehri, has tens of thousands of speakers, the others far fewer. Although they share features with ancient South Arabian languages such as Sabaic, it is now thought that they are not directly derived from them.

176 That is, the sea extends no further north.

177 Q Naml 27:61.

178 By "no kings," Abū Zayd means that there are no (civilized) kingdoms.

179 "Dismal, hostile": Arabic *muẓlim* is both "dark" and "full of difficulties, evils."

180 It was thought that ambergris exuded or grew from the seabed (cf. 1.2.1, above).

181 That is, ovoid lumps.

182 In 1.1.2, above, the similar term *wāl* may have signified the tiger shark. *Bāl* here is definitely the whale, specifically the ambergris-producing sperm whale. The substance forms in the whale's own gut, rather than being swallowed (see n. 7, above).

183 "Fishy smell" depends on a tentative reading.

184 Ibn Baṭṭūṭah (*Travels*, 2:391) also mentions houses on the southern Arabian coast built/roofed with "fish bones"; remains of such structures are still to be seen (Mackintosh-Smith, *Travels with a Tangerine*, 264). Abū Zayd's "ancient" houses are literally "ʿĀdite," that is, ascribed to the ancient people, ʿĀd.

185 The oil scooped from the whale's eye must be sperm oil, a liquid wax obtained from cavities in the sperm whale's head. The oil of the previous sentence is extracted from the blubber of various whale species. In the Gulf, the heat of the sun alone might have been enough to render it, as the text implies, without the need for heating the blubber, as practiced by whalers in cooler climates.

186 To seal gaps, the oil would of course have been used in conjunction with caulking.

187 Q Yā Sīn 36:36.

188 The comparison is with *anjudhānah*, glossed in its plural form by al-Muẓaffar (*Al-Muʿtamad*, 9) as the leaves of asafoetida, a plant with both culinary and medicinal uses. Presumably Abū Zayd or his informant was thinking of the dried leaves familiar to cooks and apothecaries of the time.

189 "Pried pearls" are what English terms "blister pearls."

190 "How God sustains His creatures in unexpected ways": more literally, "doorways/openings [that lead] to divinely provided sustenance (*rizq*)." At the end of the section, *rizq* is translated more loosely still, as "windfall."

191 *Ṣammān* in general signifies an area of low rugged hills; this particular one was nine days' journey from Basra (Yāqūt, *Muʿjam al-buldān*, 3:481). At this period, the name "Bahrain" included both the islands known by the name today and a large area of the adjacent mainland.

192 *Chatrah* (in which the text carefully specifies the consonant *ch*, alien to standard Arabic) is the Sanskrit *chattra*, "umbrella."

193 Abū Zayd's readers, when dining in company, would have eaten from communal dishes regardless of the class or status of their companions.

194 As above (see n. 83), "the sea" is shorthand for the sea itself, the islands in it, and the lands on and beyond its shores.

195 As the English saying goes, less is more.

196 Here follows a note by the copyist: "This copy was checked against the original from which it was made, in Safar of the year 596 [November–December 1199]. And God it is who guides."

Glossary of Names and Terms

ʿĀd a prehistoric proto-Arab people often mentioned in the Qurʾan.

Aden ancient trading port in the southwestern Arabian Peninsula, near the mouth of the Red Sea.

Aden and al-Qulzum, Sea of the Gulf of Aden and the Red Sea. "Al-Qulzum" is an arabicization of Clysma, the Greek name of an ancient port on the Gulf of Suez.

al-Aghbāb plural of Ghubb. See Ghubb of Sarandīb.

Andamān Sea the Andaman Islands in the Bay of Bengal are still known by the same name. The application of the name to the sea separating the islands, as in the text here, may reflect an old usage, or it may be a copyist's error.

Alexander Alexander III ("the Great"), 356–323 BC, king of Macedon and conqueror of a mainly Asian empire including Persia.

ʿanqatūs unidentified, and voweling uncertain. Al-Idrīsī (*Nuzhah*, 1:65), who drew on the present text, has *ʿanqarīs* as the name of a fish in the Sea of Lārawī.

Aristotle Greek philosopher and scientist, 384–322 BC, and tutor to Alexander (q.v.), when the latter was crown prince of Macedon.

Baghbūn an error for Baghbūr (often spelled Faghfūr), from Persian *baghpūr*, "son of the divinity" (Polo, *Travels*, 2:148 n. 1). The Arabic-speakers' (intentionally jocular?) version, al-Maghbūn, would mean "the Defrauded One, the Dupe."

baghlī dirham an early type of dirham (q.v.) supposedly named after al-Baghl, a Jewish master of the mint in the Umayyad period (Ḥibshī, *Riḥlat al-Sīrāfī*, 58 n. 1). It was modeled on the late Sasanian *drahm* (see *Encyclopaedia of Islam, Second Edition,* s.v. "Dirham"), and was a third heavier than the later standard dirham.

Balharā from Prakrit *ballaha-rāya*, "well-beloved king," a title of various monarchs in the Deccan (Sauvaget, *Relation*, 51 n. 25.1), and in particular of the second/eighth- to fourth/tenth-century dynasty known as the Rashtrakutas (Keay, *A History of India*, 157).

Bamdhū possibly a corruption of "Shamdū" but, in any case, a version of the name Chengdu, capital of Sichuan province, to which the Tang emperor Xizong removed his court during the occupation of Chang'an by Huang Chao.

Banū Kāwān Island see Ibn Kāwān Island.

Barbar by "the land of the Barbar" Abū Zayd means that of the Somalis and related people—the "Barbarah" of the Arab geographers and of Ibn Baṭṭūṭah (*Travels*, 2:373)—rather than that of the Berbers (the Arabic spelling is the same). The "Barbarī leopard skins" mentioned presumably take their name from the region of their export, not from that of their stated origin, Abyssinia. The northern Somali port of Berbera preserves the old name; Abū Zayd's "Barbarā," rather than signifying this port in particular, probably means the same as "the land of the Barbar."

Barbarā see Barbar (last sentence).

Basra city in southeastern Iraq, on the Shaṭṭ al-ʿArab waterway.

bīkarjī seemingly a garbled and arabicized version of Sanskrit *vairāgika*, "ascetic," or some derivation from it. Cf. also the note on *bīkūr/baykūr* in al-Rāmhurmuzī, *ʿAjāʾib al-hind*, 194–95.

budd from Persian *but*, "idol."

bushān probably from Sanskrit *viṣāna*, "horn."

bussadh (spelled *busadd* in the manuscript) preferred by al-Bīrūnī, in his book on precious stones (*Kitāb al-jamāhir*, 137), to the more common *murjān* as the term for coral.

Dahmā a emendation of the manuscript's "Ruhmā." "Dahmā" is, in turn, a plausible arabicization and shortening of *Dharma-pāla*, title of a king prominent in northern India in the early ninth century.

dahnaj the deep-green copper-bearing mineral malachite (Persian *dahnah*).

darā a Persian word for "bell."

Darius the Great here referring to Darius III, the last Achaemenid ruler of Persia (r. 336–330). "The Great" is more usually the epithet of Darius I.

al-Dībājāt Islands the archipelagos of the Maldives and Laccadives (Lakshadweep) in the Arabian Sea. "1900" is too many; the actual number is between 1200 and 1300.

dīfū Chinese *tai fu*, title of a high-ranking governor (Sauvaget, *Relation*, 58 n. 37.2).

dinar the standard gold coin, for many centuries, of much of the Islamic world. Its official weight was about 4.25 grams.

dirham the standard silver coin, for many centuries, of much of the Islamic world. Its weight varied between 2.5 grams and 3 grams.

Dualists known also as Manicheans, from the name of the founder of their religion, Mani (third century AD). Their dualism was a belief in a primeval and eternal conflict between the powers of light and darkness.

fafaghā cognate with the standard Arabic word for a parrot, *bab[b]aghā'* (used in the text in a plural form, *babbaghāwāt*, to gloss it), and perhaps a dialect variant.

fakkūj a term, of uncertain origin, for a string of one thousand copper "cash." It was worth, according to Book Two (2.3.3), about a *mithqāl* of gold—a weight equal to that of one dinar. This corresponds approximately with the Chinese silver equivalent in value, the *liang* (Yule and Burnell, *Hobson-Jobson*, s.v. "Tael"). Professor Zvi Ben-Dor Benite suggests that *fakkūj* may be a distortion of *fang kongqian*, a generic term for "cash" in premodern China (personal communication).

Fanṣūr the region of Barus, on the west coast of Sumatra (cf. Tibbetts, *Arab Navigation*, 490).

al-Faqīr Muḥammad unknown. *Al-faqīr* is, in general, a pious epithet—"he who is in need [of God's mercy]"—and was used by Sufis leading lives of poverty.

farsakh a linear measure (Persian *parasang*) of about 5.77 kilometers but varying considerably according to local usage (Ibn Baṭṭūṭah, *Travels*, 1:34 n. 93).

fils any small copper coin, including the Chinese currency known as "cash."

Fire, Mount of it is impossible to know which of the many active volcanoes in the Indonesian Archipelago is intended here.

Gates of China the Paracel Islands, a group of low-lying coral islands and reefs in the South China Sea, now administered by China.

Ghubb of Sarandīb the editors of al-Rāmhurmuzī discuss (*ʿAjāʾib*, 274–75) the identity of the (plural) Ghubbs of Sarandīb mentioned in that work but do not locate them any more precisely than in the Coromandel region of southeastern India, in the modern states of Andhra Pradesh and Tamil Nadu. The great length of the Ghubb in our text—two months' travel—suggests a network of waterways; if a single river is meant, it may be the Cauvery, which is more than 750 kilometers long.

Habbār ibn al-Aswad a tribesman of Quraysh (q.v.), who was a contemporary and a distant cousin of the Prophet Muḥammad.

hadith accounts of the utterances and deeds of the Prophet Muḥammad and his Companions.

ḥarām probably from Sanskrit *ārāma*, "garden" (cf. *jarām* in al-Rāmhurmuzī, *ʿAjāʾib*, 195).

Harkand, Sea of the Bay of Bengal.

Ḥimyar name of a South Arabian people and of the last indigenous power to rule Yemen before the coming of Islam.

Huang Chao in the manuscript "Bānshū," probably an error for "Yānshū." Leader of a rebellion (874–84) that seriously weakened the power of the Tang Dynasty. Although the rebellion was eventually put down, the Tang never fully recovered.

Ibn Kāwān Island the Iranian island of Qishm (Tibbetts, *Arab Navigation*, 447), south of Bandar ʿAbbās and west of the Strait of Hormuz. The name is the usual Arabic deformation of the island's pre-Islamic name, Abarkāwān (Sauvaget, *Relation*, 42 n. 13.5). On occasion, the name appears, further deformed, as "Banū Kāwān."

Ibn Wahb al-Qurashī traveler from Basra, known only from this text and others deriving from it.

jādam modern Chinese *haotong*, "signaling tube," Tibetan *r gyadung* (Sauvaget, *Relation*, 56 n. 33.3).

Jalīdiyyah see Kanīfiyyah.

al-Jār former Red Sea port, now the site of the city of Yanbuʿ, in present-day Saudi Arabia.

jazbī voweling conjectural. This may represent a non-Arabic word; other possible readings include *jurbī*, which could conceivably be a corruption of *jurī*/*churī*, the latter being the Sanskrit word for "knife." (The Sanskrit term is arabicized by al-Masʿūdī, *Murūj*, 1:210, as *jurīʾ*.) However, because the verb *jazaba* is a southern Arabian dialect variant of standard Arabic *jazama*, "to cut, lop" (Piamenta, *Dictionary*, s.v. *jazama*), and *jazbī* would be a plausible formation from it, it is also possible that the term here is an Arabic one.

Jidda Red Sea port in present-day Saudi Arabia, the nearest seaport to Mecca.

Jurhum ancient South Arabian tribe, who, for a time, controlled pre-Islamic Mecca.

al-Jurz the Gurjaras. By the mid-ninth century, the Gurjaras controlled much of northern India. The reference to their king inhabiting a peninsula—literally, "a tongue of land"—may refer to the original Gurjara homelands, which included, along with the Indus Valley, the Kathiawar Peninsula.

kabtaj this may be a version of some word cognate with the Sanskrit name for the cowry, *kaparda* (Yule and Burnell, *Hobson-Jobson*, s.v. "Cowry"). Van Der Lith and Devic discuss the word at length (al-Rāmhurmuzī, *ʿAjāʾib*, 216–17) but inconclusively.

Kalah, Peninsula of the Malay Peninsula, or some portion of it, and the location of Kalah Bār (q.v.). Opinions probably varied at different periods as to whether it was a peninsula or an island (Arabic *jazīrah* can serve for both).

Kalah Bār on the west coast of the Malay Peninsula. Its exact location is unknown, but a form of the first part of the name may survive in that of the Malaysian state of Kedah. "Bār" derives ultimately from Sanskrit *vāra*, "district."

Kanduranj this seems to be a version of "Panduranga," the modern Phan Rang, a major city of the kingdom of Champa, located on the south coast of Vietnam.

Kanīfiyyah this and the associated term Jalīdiyyah probably refer to two rival gangs in Iraq. Ḥibshī (*Riḥlat al-Sīrāfī*, 79 n. 2) suggests amending the reading of the former to "Katīfiyyah" and deriving it from *katīf*, a broad-bladed sword; the second term he associates (79 n. 3) with the verb *jālada*, "to fight with a sword." Following Ḥibshī, the terms might thus be rendered "the Broadswordsmen" and "the Fencers." Equally tentative is a reference in Bosworth (*The Mediaeval Islamic Underworld*, 1:43–44 n. 117) to the two gangs (whose names are, however, read slightly differently) as "the Khulaidiyya, 'those condemned to perpetual imprisonment' (?), mentioned [by al-Jāḥiẓ] as a group of beggars or brigands . . . and linked with the Katīfiyya/Kutaifiyya, perhaps those chained up by their shoulders (*aktāf*) or in irons (*katā'if*)." There are, however, other possible derivations (*kanīf* is, inter alia, "a lavatory"; *jalīd*, applied to a person, means "tough").

al-Kāshibīn Ferrand takes this as a corruption of Lakṣmipura, the name of a town in eastern Assam (Sauvaget, *Relation*, 54 n. 29.1).

Khamdān the usual Arabic version of the name of the Tang Dynasty imperial capital, Chang'an, now called Xi'an.

Khānfū the Chinese city of Guangzhou. The Arabic name probably reflects a shortened version of the old official name of the city, Guangzhou-fu (Yule and Burnell, *Hobson-Jobson*, s.v. "Canton").

khāqān a Turkic royal title. Its application to the ruler of Tibet shows that information about that country arrived via Turkic intermediaries.

kharābāt specified by Tibbetts (*Arab Navigation*, 55) as "anchor ropes." The term is still in use.

Khazars, Sea of the the Caspian Sea. The Khazars were a Turkic people living in the lower Volga basin.

Khurasan a large province in northeastern Iran.

al-Khushnāmī unidentified. The word is from Persian and means "of good name."

Kisrā title of the pre-Islamic Persian kings, arabicized from "Khusraw."

Kūlam Malī Kollam, in the Indian state of Kerala.

al-Kumkum Sanskrit Konkaṇa, the low-lying part of the western coast of India between Goa and Gujarat (Yule and Burnell, *Hobson-Jobson*, s.v. "Concan").

Kusayr and ʿUwayr Yāqūt (*Muʿjam*, s.v. "Kusayr") points out that the names of these dangerous rocks are derived from the words for "breaking" and "spoiling." They belong to a group of islets lying off the tip of the Musandam Peninsula and known as "Salāmah and her Daughters" (Ibn Baṭṭūṭah, *Travels*, 1:409–10 n. 144).

Lanjabālūs Islands the Nicobar Islands.

laqshī mamkūn a slightly deformed arabicization of Chinese *lüshicanjun* (Professor Zvi Ben-Dor Benite, personal communication). Professor Benite adds that there is a confusion in our text over the nature of this office, which, under the Tang Dynasty, was associated with a military rather than a judicial function.

Lārawī, Sea of the Gulf of Oman and the northern part of the Arabian Sea.

lashak possibly from a non-Arabic word, but cf. the later Arabic name for the remora fish, *luzzāq*, connected with the verb *laziqa*, "to stick" (Tibbetts, *Arab Navigation*, 288). As reflected by another of its English names, "shark sucker," the remora does attach itself to sharks, but its relationship with them tends to be commensal, not destructive.

līkhū Sauvaget (*Relation*, 59 n. 38.4) reads *lnjūn*, with the first letter unvocalized, and equates with a title given to high-level secretaries.

lukham sharks in all their varieties.

al-Mābud reading conjectural. Sauvaget (*Relation*, 55 n. 32.1) derives the name from Tibetan *smad bod*, a term for the eastern part of Tibet.

Madīnat al-Salām "The City of Security, of Peace," an alternative name for Baghdad.

Maghbūn see Baghbūn.

Magians that is, Zoroastrians. The comparison in the text between Chinese and Zoroastrian beliefs reflects the hazy notions many Muslims held about the latter.

Maljān Island unidentified, and first vowel uncertain. Sauvaget (*Relation*, 46 n. 18.1) suggests a connection with the name of the Mergui

Archipelago, off the coast of Burma. Perhaps more evocative of the Arabic is the name of the largest island in the group, Mali Kyun.

mand al-Muẓaffar (*Al-Muʿtamad*, 339 and 340) lists *mandah* as low-grade, black ambergris used to adulterate the more valuable grades.

al-Manṣūrah founded as their capital in the second/eighth century by the Muslim conquerors of Sind, it was located in southern present-day Pakistan.

al-Mihrāj voweled thus in the manuscript. An arabicization, probably via Persian, of the Indian title "Maharaja." The rulers referred to here are probably those of the Sailendra kingdom, based in Java between the first/seventh and fifth/eleventh centuries.

mīj a Persian word for "locust" (Sauvaget, *Relation*, 34 n. 3.1). The Arabic name *jarād al-baḥr*, "sea locusts," sometimes applied elsewhere to prawns/shrimps, is used in southern Arabia for flying fish (Tibbetts, *Arab Navigation*, 286 n. 74).

mithqāl a unit of weight equivalent to that of a dinar (q.v.).

Muḍar in traditional genealogy, the progenitor of an eponymous major tribe, one of the two main branches of the so-called ʿAdnānī or Northern Arabs; the other branch is named for Rabīʿah.

al-Mūjah apparently the ethnic group known in Chinese as the Miao, or Miaozhu, found in southern China and neighboring regions (Professor Zvi Ben-Dor Benite, personal communication).

al-Mūltān (usual later Arabic form "Multān") Multan, an ancient city in central present-day Pakistan. The phrase in the text could be understood as "the [well-]known idol of al-Mūltān," but it seems more likely that Abū Zayd regarded the name as that of the idol first (and the place second). The idol in question was a representation of the solar deity Surya or Aditya (al-Bīrūnī, *Albêrûnî's India*, 100).

al-Niyān Island Pulau Nias, called locally Tanö Niha, off the west coast of Sumatra.

al-Qamār the usual Arabic name in old texts for the region including present-day Cambodia. It is cognate with the name of the most prominent people of the region, the Khmer.

Qāmarūn the Kamrup region of Assam (cf. Ibn Baṭṭūṭah's "Kāmarū," *Travels*, 4:869).

Qannawj Kannauj, on the Ganges, in present-day Uttar Pradesh.

al-Qulzum see Aden and al-Qulzum, Sea of.

Quraysh Arab tribe centered on Mecca, to which the Prophet Muḥammad belonged.

al-Qyrnj voweling and interpretation uncertain; possibly located in what is now Burma (Myanmar).

Rabīʿah in traditional genealogy, the progenitor of an eponymous major tribe, one of the two main branches of the so-called ʿAdnānī or Northern Arabs; the other branch is named for Muḍar.

al-Rahūn Sripada or Adam's Peak, a mountain and pilgrimage site in Sri Lanka. Cf. Ruhuna Raṭa, the ancient Pali name for southern Sri Lanka (Skeen, *Adam's Peak*, 22).

al-Rāmanī Island seemingly a corruption of "Lāmurī" (or some variant), the name of a port in or near the Aceh region of Sumatra but applied by early writers to Sumatra as a whole (al-Tājir, *Akhbār al-ṣīn wa-l-hind*, 104–5).

al-Rūm, Gulf of "The Gulf of the Romans/Byzantines," which, in Abū Zayd's hazy understanding, appears to include not only the Bosphorus, the Sea of Marmara, and the Dardanelles but also the Black Sea and the Sea of Azov.

sākh the passage here describing it is the first correct foreign mention of tea. As it stands, the Arabic name is presumably a corruption of the Chinese *cha* (or some dialect variant). The original Arabic form may have been (by simple rearrangement of dots) *shāj*, with the *j* pronounced, as it is in several Gulf dialects, as a *y*; cf. the later standard Arabic *shāy*.

Salāhiṭ, Sea of the Malacca Strait. From *selat*, the Malay term for "strait" (Hourani, *Arab Seafaring*, 71).

ṣamar at first sight, from Sanskrit *camara*, "fly whisk." The traditional *camara*, however, is made from a yak's tail, so other explanations may be in order.

Samarqand ancient trading city of Sogdiana (q.v.), now the second-largest city in Uzbekistan.

Ṣandar Fūlāt Sauvaget (*Relation*, 45–46 n. 16.4) sees this as a copyist's error for (although it may be a mariners' version of) the name Ṣanf Fūlāw, "the island of Champa," Fūlāw representing *pulau*, the Malay word for "island." Possibly one of the Vietnamese group still known as Cu Lao Cham, "the Cham[pa] Islands," near the mainland port of Hoi An, or the island of Ly Son, about one hundred kilometers to the southeast.

Ṣanf the Arabic approximation of "Champa," the name of the ancient kingdom in the coastal region of what is now Vietnam. The text seems to indicate a particular port by the name, but its location is unclear. The main port of Champa in the central coastal region of Vietnam was near the present-day town of Quy Nhon.

Ṣankhī, Sea of the northern part of the South China Sea. Probably from Chinese *san hai*, "huge sea."

Sarandīb the most common name for Sri Lanka in early Arabic texts.

Sarbuzah voweled thus by Yāqūt (*Muʿjam*). Its location has been much discussed, especially by the editors of al-Rāmhurmuzī (*ʿAjāʾib*, 247–53), who identify it with Palembang, in southeastern Sumatra. Given that Sumatra is already represented in our text by the island of al-Rāmanī and that Sarbuzah is itself said to be a large island, it should perhaps be sought elsewhere. Borneo has also been suggested as a possibility. At the risk of adding to the confusion, Sulawesi, on the grounds both of its name and its size, might also be a contender.

al-Sha'm otherwise written al-Shām and translated elsewhere as "the Levant." In the context of a description of the Red Sea and neighboring coasts, "the coast of al-Sha'm" must refer to the Gulf of Aqaba.

al-Shiḥr now the name of a town on the south coast of Yemen but formerly denoting a region including much of the southern coast of the Arabian Peninsula and its hinterland.

Sīf Banī l-Ṣaffāq a coastal region (*sīf*, meaning "shore") in southern Iran, between Sīrāf (q.v.) and Qishm (see Ibn Kāwān Island, above) (Bosworth, "The Nomenclature of the Persian Gulf," 83). Yāqūt has "Sīf Banī l-Ṣaffār" (*Muʿjam*).

al-Sīlā the early Arabic name for Korea, from the Silla dynasty who ruled it until the tenth century AD. The reference to Korea as "islands" might be translated as "peninsula and adjoining islands," but, as the text implies, notions of the country's geography were hazy.

Silver, Islands of unidentified.

sindī dinars dinars (q.v.) of Sind, which is, properly speaking, the territory on the Indus below the Punjab (Yule and Burnell, *Hobson-Jobson*, s.v. "Sind"). Exactly what coins are intended is unclear, although large gold coins were used in the area before the Islamic period, and the imported coinage may have catered to local tastes.

Sīrāf until its near-destruction by an earthquake in 366-67/977 (Hourani, *Arab Seafaring*, 78) the chief port on the Iranian side of the Arabian/Persian Gulf, south of Shīrāz. Sīrāf was the origin of Abū Zayd, author of the second part of this work.

al-Sīrāfī, Abū Zayd al-Ḥasan see Introduction, 6–7.

Socotra (also written in English as Soqotra and Suqutra) The largest island in the Arab world, belonging to Yemen and lying off the Horn of Africa.

Sogdiana ancient name for a Central Asian land east of Khurasan (q.v.) and centered on Samarqand (q.v.).

Sulaymān the Merchant although the single mention of him in the earlier part of the text suggests that he was an informant, Sulaymān al-Tājir ("the Merchant") was credited by the geographer Ibn al-Faqīh as its author or compiler (al-Tājir, *Akhbār*, 11 and 12). More recent commentators have disagreed with this ascription. See also Introduction, 5.

Taghazghuz voweled thus in the manuscript. An arabicization of the Turkic name Toquz Oghuz, "the Nine Oghuz [Tribes]," a group including the Turkic people known today as Uighurs.

Tamīm in traditional genealogy, a descendant of Muḍar (q.v.). In the text, the name is used as an alternative to Muḍar as a tribal name.

al-Ṭāqā the manuscript has "al-Ṭāfiq." Al-Ṭāqā is Sauvaget's suggested emendation (*Relation*, 52 n.27.1); it may reflect "Ṭakka," the name in Indian sources of a kingdom in the upper reaches of the Chenab and Ravi rivers.

ṭāṭirī dirhams the phrase is repeated by other authorities who have drawn on this text, but there is no convincing explanation for it. Yule and Burnell (*Hobson-Jobson*, 896) cite *tetari* as a Mingrelian term for a silver coin. The reference here could be to the coinage of the Shahi dynasty of Kabul and Gandhara, often imitated at this period by other North Indian kingdoms, its standard silver denomination being, as the text suggests, considerably heavier than the Islamic dirham.

al-Tāyin (the "i" is conjectural) unidentified.

Tāyū identified by Sauvaget (*Relation*, 62 n. 49.1) as Taihu, in southwest Anhui province. Later reports of alleged Chinese "pygmies" include one, emanating from approximately this region of China, in the purported travels of Sir John Mandeville (Moseley, *Travels*, 139–40).

thalāj first vowel conjectural. As used in the text, the word signifies the tidal reach of a river, or a tidal basin. An arabicization derived ultimately from Sanskrit *talāga*, explained by the editors of al-Rāmhurmuzī (*ʿAjāʾib*, 195) as "lagoon"; cf. also modern Indonesian *telaga*, "lake, pond."

Tiyūmah Island Tioman, now part of the southeastern Malaysian state of Pahang.

Tubbaʿ a personal name (but considered by later Arab writers to be a title) of some of the later kings of Ḥimyar (q.v.).

Tubbat Tibet.

ṭūqām Chinese *tujian*, director-in-chief of the eunuch hierarchy (Professor Zvi Ben-Dor Benite, personal communication).

ṭūsanj Professor Zvi Ben-Dor Benite suggests that this may represent the second and third elements of the longer term *jieduzhangshuzhi*, "a versatile and ubiquitous title" that came, in post-Tang times, to mean "prefectural secretary" (personal communication).

wāl cf. *awāl/afāl* in al-Masʿūdī (*Murūj*, 1:108), often assumed to be a whale. In view of the information given here (and allowing for some exaggeration in measurement) the tiger shark, which can exceed six meters in length, might be a likelier candidate.

yasārah feasibly a corruption of *bas[h]ārah*, which might, in turn, be an arabicization (with metathesis) of a word derived from *varṣā*, Sanskrit for "rain"; this suggestion is, however, highly tentative. Because both *yasārah* and *bashārah* have meanings in Arabic—"ease of living" and "good tidings," respectively—what might be called "semantic assimilation" may be involved here. Al-Masʿūdī (*Murūj*, 1:148) uses the same term and mentions a verb derived from it, *yassara*, "to spend the rainy season."

al-Zābaj Java. The name is probably an arabicized version of the early form "Jāwaga" (Yule, *Cathay*, 1:127 n. 6).

Zanj the usual Arabic word for the black peoples of East Africa south of the equator.

al-Zaylaʿ usually Zaylaʿ; also spelled Zeila. Town on the northern coast of Somalia, near the border with Djibouti, formerly the principal port of the region.

Bibliography

Adūnīs [Adonis]. *Al-Thābit wa-l-mutaḥawwil.* 10th ed. 4 vols. Beirut: Dār al-Sāqī, 2011.

Bīrūnī, Abū Rayḥān Muḥammad ibn Aḥmad al-. *Albêrûnî's India.* Translated by Edward C. Sachau. New Delhi: Rupa, 2002. Originally published London: Trübner, 1888.

Bīrūnī, Abū Rayḥān Muḥammad ibn Aḥmad al-. *Kitāb al-Jamāhir fī maʿrifat al-jawāhir.* Beirut: ʿĀlam al-Kutub, 1984.

Bosworth, Clifford Edmund. *The Mediaeval Islamic Underworld.* 2 vols. Leiden: E.J. Brill, 1976.

Bosworth, Clifford Edmund. "The Nomenclature of the Persian Gulf." *Iranian Studies* 30, nos. 1/2 (1997): 77–94.

Cheung, Catherine, and Lyndon DeVantier. *Socotra: A Natural History of the Islands and Their People.* Hong Kong: Odyssey Books and Guides, 2006.

Elliot, H.M., and J. Dowson. *The History of India as Told by its Own Historians.* London: Trübner, 1867.

Encyclopaedia of Islam, Second Edition, edited by H.A.R. Gibb et al. 13 vols. Leiden: E.J. Brill, 1960–2009.

Ḥibshī, ʿAbdallāh al-, ed. *Riḥlat al-Sīrāfī.* Abu Dhabi: al-Mujammaʿ al-Thaqāfī, 1999.

Hourani, George F. *Arab Seafaring in the Indian Ocean in Ancient and Early Medieval Times.* Revised and expanded by John Carswell. Princeton: Princeton University Press, 1995.

Ibn Baṭṭūṭah, Muḥammad ibn ʿAbdallāh. *The Travels of Ibn Baṭṭūṭa: A.D. 1325–1354.* Translated by H.A.R. Gibb and C.F. Beckingham. 4 vols. London: Hakluyt Society, 1958–94.

Idrīsī, Muḥammad ibn Muḥammad al-. *Kitāb Nuzhat al-mushtāq fī ikhtirāq al-āfāq*. 2 vols. Cairo: Maktabat al-Thaqāfah al-Dīniyyah, n.d.

Keay, John. *A History of India*. London: HarperCollins, 2000.

Lane, Edward William. *Madd al-qāmūs: An Arabic-English Lexicon*. 8 vols. New Delhi: Asian Educational Services, 1985. Originally published London: Williams and Norgate, 1863–93.

Mackintosh-Smith, Tim. *Travels with a Tangerine: A Journey in the Footnotes of Ibn Battutah*. London: John Murray, 2001.

Mackintosh-Smith, Tim. *Landfalls: On the Edge of Islam with Ibn Battutah*. London: John Murray, 2010.

Masʿūdī, ʿAlī ibn al-Ḥusyan al-. *Murūj al-dhahab wa-maʿādin al-jawhar*. Edited by Muḥammad Muḥyī l-Dīn ʿAbd al-Ḥamīd. 4 vols. Beirut: Dār al-Maʿrifah, n.d.

Miquel, André. *Géographie humaine du monde musulman*. 2nd ed. 2 vols. Paris: Mouton, 1973.

Morris, Jan. *Hong Kong*. New York: Vintage Books, 1989. Originally published London: Penguin, 1988.

Moseley, C. W. R. D., ed. and trans. *The Travels of Sir John Mandeville*. London: Penguin, 1983.

Muẓaffar al-Ghassānī, Yūsuf ibn ʿUmar ibn ʿAlī ibn Rasūl al-Malik al-. *Al-Muʿtamad fī l-adwiyah al-mufradah*. Edited by Muṣṭafā al-Saqqā. Beirut: Dār al-Maʿrifah, n.d.

Pellat, Charles, ed. and trans. (into French). *The Life and Works of Jāḥiẓ*. Translated (into English) by D. M. Hawke. London: Routledge and Kegan Paul, 1969.

Piamenta, Moshe. *Dictionary of Post-Classical Yemeni Arabic*. 2 vols. Leiden: E. J. Brill, 1990.

Polo, Marco. *The Travels of Marco Polo*. Translated and annotated by Henry Yule (3rd ed., revised by Henri Cordier). 2 vols. New York: Dover Publications Inc., 1993. Originally published London: John Murray, 1929.

Rāmhurmuzī, Buzurg ibn Shahriyār al-. *ʿAjāʾib al-hind*. Edited by P. A. Van Der Lith and translated by L. Marcel Devic. Leiden: E. J. Brill, 1883–86.

Reinaud, Joseph Toussaint, ed. and trans. *Relation des voyages faits par les Arabes et les Persans dans l'Inde et à la Chine* (Arabic text originally edited by Louis-Mathieu Langlès). 2 vols. Paris: Imprimerie Royale, 1845.

Renaudot, Eusèbe, trans. (into French; English trans. from French by anon.). *Ancient Accounts of India and China by Two Mohammedan Travellers, Who Went to Those Parts in the 9th Century*. London: Samuel Harding, 1733.

Sauvaget, Jean, ed. and trans. *Relation de la Chine et de l'Inde, rédigée en 851*. Paris: Belles Lettres, 1948.

Serjeant, R. B., and Ronald Lewcock, eds. *Ṣanʿāʾ: An Arabian Islamic City*. London: World of Islam Festival Trust, 1983.

Severin, Tim. *The Sindbad Voyage*. London: Hutchinson 1982.

Skeen, William. *Adam's Peak*. New Delhi: Asian Educational Services, 1997. Originally published Colombo: W. L. H. Skeen, 1870.

Tājir, Sulaymān al- (attributed) and Abū Zayd al-Sīrāfī. *Akhbār al-ṣīn wa-l-hind*. Edited by Ibrāhīm Khūrī. Beirut: Dār al-Mawsim li-l-Iʿlām, 1411/1991.

Tennent, James Emerson. *Ceylon*. 2 vols. New Delhi: Asian Educational Services, 1999. Originally published London: Longman, Green, Longman, and Roberts, 1859.

Tibbetts, G. R. *Arab Navigation in the Indian Ocean Before the Coming of the Portuguese*. London: Royal Asiatic Society, 1971.

Whitehouse, David. "Siraf: A Medieval Port on the Persian Gulf." *World Archaeology* 2, no. 2 (October 1970): 141–58.

Whitfield, Susan. *Life Along the Silk Road*. London: John Murray, 2000. Originally published London: John Murray, 1999.

Yāqūt al-Ḥamawī, *Muʿjam al-buldān*. Edited by Farīd ʿAbd al-ʿAzīz al-Jundī. 7 vols. Beirut: Dār al-Kutub al-ʿIlmiyyah, n.d.

Yule, Henry. *Cathay and the Way Thither*. 2nd edition. Revised by Henri Cordier. 4 vols. New Delhi: Munshiram Manoharlal, 1998. Originally published London: The Hakluyt Society, 1916.

Yule, Henry, and A. C. Burnell. *Hobson-Jobson: The Anglo-Indian Dictionary*. 2nd ed. Edited by W. Crooke. Ware, UK: Wordsworth, 1996. Originally published London: John Murray, 1903.

Zhang Jun-yan. "Relations between China and the Arabs in Early Times." *Journal of Oman Studies* 6, no. 1 (1983): 91–109.

Index

Abbasid caliph, xxvi; dynasty, xxxi
ʿAbīd ibn Sharyah, xxiii
Abū Zayd al-Ḥasan al-Sīrāfī, xix–xx, xxii–xxviii, §2.1.1, §2.19.1, 80n102, 81n118, 83n144, 84n146, 84n155, 86n173, 86n178, 86n184, 87n188, 87n193; his evaluation of the First Book of *Accounts of China and India*, §2.1.1
Abyssinia, xxi, §2.15.2
Accounts of China and India, authorship, xviii–xxi; contents, xi, xxiv; dating, xviii–xxi; informants, xii, xix–xxi; linguistic features, xxiv, xxix–xxx; manuscript, xviii, xxx; previous translations, xiii, xxx; structure; used by later authors, xxviii–xxix; used by al-Masʿūdī, xxvi–xxviii
ʿĀd, §2.15.2, 86n184
Adam, §1.2.2
Adam's Peak, 84n153. *See also* al-Rahūn
Aden, §2.15.2
Aden and al-Qulzum, Sea of, §2.5.1
"Ādite' dialects, §2.15.2. *See also* Modern South Arabian language group
adultery, §1.10.2, §2.3.1, §2.7.1
al-Aghbāb, §§2.11.1–2.11.6. *See also* Ghubb of Sarandīb
Aḥmad ibn Mājid, 74n32
ʿAjāʾib al-hind. *See Wonders of India*
akhbār literature, xviii, xx, xxiii–xxiv
Akhbār al-ṣīn wa-l-hind. *See Accounts of China and India*
Alexander the Great, §2.2.3, §2.14.1, 79n90, 86n172
ʿAlī ibn Abī Ṭālib, 79n92
aloes, §1.8.4, §2.14.1, 75n54, 85n168
aloewood, xvii, §1.2.2, §1.4.5, §1.7.5, §2.6.1, §2.7.1, §2.15.5, §2.15.3, 72n13
ambergris, xvii, xxi, §1.2.1, §1.2.5, §1.2.7, §1.4.3, §1.7.7, §2.5.1, §2.15.2, §2.15.3, §2.16.1, 71n7, 74n43, 86n180, 86n182
Andaman Islands, Andamān Sea, §1.2.5
Angel of Death, §1.9.2
Aqaba, Gulf of, §2.15.2
Arabian/Persian Gulf, xix, xxi–xxiii, §1.3.3, 71n2, 73n26, 73n28, 73n29, 76n61, 87n185
Arabs, xxi, xxiii, xxv–xxvi, xxviii, §§1.3.1–1.3.3, §1.4.3, §§1.7.1–1.7.4, §1.8.4, §1.8.7, §1.8.9, §1.10.8, §1.10.10, §2.2.1, §2.2.3, §2.3.3, §2.3.5, §§2.4.1–2.4.4, §2.5.1, §2.6.1,

About the NYU Abu Dhabi Institute

The Library of Arabic Literature is supported by a grant from the NYU Abu Dhabi Institute, a major hub of intellectual and creative activity and advanced research. The Institute hosts academic conferences, workshops, lectures, film series, performances, and other public programs directed both to audiences within the UAE and to the worldwide academic and research community. It is a center of the scholarly community for Abu Dhabi, bringing together faculty and researchers from institutions of higher learning throughout the region.

NYU Abu Dhabi, through the NYU Abu Dhabi Institute, is a world-class center of cutting-edge research, scholarship, and cultural activity. The Institute creates singular opportunities for leading researchers from across the arts, humanities, social sciences, sciences, engineering, and the professions to carry out creative scholarship and conduct research on issues of major disciplinary, multidisciplinary, and global significance.

About the Translator

Tim Mackintosh-Smith is an independent scholar specializing in Arabic travel literature and is the author of several books of his own travels. Of these, his trilogy on Ibn Baṭṭūṭah (*Travels with a Tangerine*, *The Hall of a Thousand Columns*, and *Landfalls*) retraces the fourteenth-century Moroccan's journeys across three continents. His work has earned him the 1998 Thomas Cook/*Daily Telegraph* Travel Book Award and, appropriately, the Ibn Baṭṭūṭah Prize of Honour, awarded in 2010 by the Arab Centre for Geographical Literature. He has been based for over thirty years in the Yemeni capital, Sanaa.

The Library of Arabic Literature

For more details on individual titles, visit www.libraryofarabicliterature.org.

Classical Arabic Literature: A Library of Arabic Literature Anthology
Selected and translated by Geert Jan van Gelder

A Treasury of Virtues: Sayings, Sermons and Teachings of ʿAlī, by al-Qāḍī al-Quḍāʿī with the *One Hundred Proverbs* attributed to al-Jāḥiẓ
Edited and translated by Tahera Qutbuddin

The Epistle on Legal Theory, by al-Shāfiʿī
Edited and translated by Joseph E. Lowry

Leg over Leg, by Aḥmad Fāris al-Shidyāq
Edited and translated by Humphrey Davies

Virtues of the Imām Aḥmad ibn Ḥanbal, by Ibn al-Jawzī
Edited and translated by Michael Cooperson

The Epistle of Forgiveness, by Abū l-ʿAlāʾ al-Maʿarrī
Edited and translated by Geert Jan van Gelder and Gregor Schoeler

The Principles of Sufism, by ʿĀʾishah al-Bāʿūniyyah
Edited and translated by Th. Emil Homerin

The Expeditions: An Early Biography of Muḥammad, by Maʿmar ibn Rāshid
Edited and translated by Sean W. Anthony

Two Arabic Travel Books
Accounts of China and India, by Abū Zayd al-Sīrāfī
Edited and translated by Tim Mackintosh-Smith

Mission to the Volga, by Aḥmad ibn Faḍlān
Edited and translated by James Montgomery

Disagreements of the Jurists: A Manual of Islamic Legal Theory, by al-Qāḍī al-Nuʿmān
Edited and translated by Devin J. Stewart

Consorts of the Caliphs: Women and the Court of Baghdad, by Ibn al-Sāʿī
Edited by Shawkat M. Toorawa and translated by the Editors of the Library of Arabic Literature

What ʿĪsā ibn Hishām Told Us, by Muḥammad al-Muwayliḥī
Edited and translated by Roger Allen

The Life and Times of Abū Tammām, by Abū Bakr Muḥammad ibn Yaḥyā al-Ṣūlī
Edited and translated by Beatrice Gruendler

The Sword of Ambition: Bureaucratic Rivalry in Medieval Egypt, by ʿUthmān ibn Ibrāhīm al-Nābulusī
Edited and translated by Luke Yarbrough

Brains Confounded by the Ode of Abū Shādūf Expounded, by Yūsuf al-Shirbīnī
Edited and translated by Humphrey Davies

Light in the Heavens: Sayings of the Prophet Muḥammad, by al-Qāḍī al-Quḍāʿī
Edited and translated by Tahera Qutbuddin

Risible Rhymes, by Muḥammad ibn Maḥfūẓ al-Sanhūrī
Edited and translated by Humphrey Davies

A Hundred and One Nights
Edited and translated by Bruce Fudge

The Excellence of the Arabs, by Ibn Qutaybah
Edited by James E. Montgomery and Peter Webb
Translated by Sarah Bowen Savant and Peter Webb

Scents and Flavors: A Syrian Cookbook
Edited and translated by Charles Perry

English-only Paperbacks

Leg over Leg: Volumes One and Two, by Aḥmad Fāris al-Shidyāq

Leg over Leg: Volumes Three and Four, by Aḥmad Fāris al-Shidyāq

The Expeditions: An Early Biography of Muḥammad, by Maʿmar ibn Rāshid

The Epistle on Legal Theory: A Translation of al-Shāfiʿī's Risālah, by al-Shāfiʿī

The Epistle of Forgiveness, by Abū l-ʿAlāʾ al-Maʿarrī

The Principles of Sufism, by ʿĀʾishah al-Bāʿūniyyah

A Treasury of Virtues: Sayings, Sermons and Teachings of ʿAlī, by al-Qāḍī al-Quḍāʿī with *The One Hundred Proverbs*, attributed to al-Jāḥiẓ

The Life of Ibn Ḥanbal, by Ibn al-Jawzī

Mission to the Volga, by Ibn Faḍlān

Accounts of China and India, by Abū Zayd al-Sīrāfī